T0368359

MY CANCER JOURNEY AND LESSONS LEARNED

A BOOK OF DEVOTIONS

LINDA MORGAN ANDERSON

WESTBOW
PRESS®
A DIVISION OF THOMAS NELSON
& ZONDERVAN

WestBow Press books may be ordered through booksellers or by contacting:

WestBow Press
A Division of Thomas Nelson & Zondervan
1663 Liberty Drive
Bloomington, IN 47403
www.westbowpress.com
844-714-3454

ISBN: 979-8-3850-3679-0 (sc)
ISBN: 979-8-3850-3680-6 (hc)
ISBN: 979-8-3850-3681-3 (e)

Library of Congress Control Number: 2024922150

Print information available on the last page.

WestBow Press rev. date: 03/12/2025

DEDICATION

This book is dedicated to all those who have dealt with cancer themselves or with family members and close friends. Cancer is not something that anyone wants to have, but when it occurs, we need to turn to the only one who can walk with us through these difficult times. I found through my faith that God has been my constant companion. I hope these devotions give those who read them strength for today and hope for tomorrow.

I also dedicate this book to my wonderful husband Norm Anderson who has been by my side from that first day in my primary care doctor's office as she looked at my lab results. We watched the color go from her face as she studied the results. Then two days later we walked down the hallway to my oncologist's office, a walk I never dreamed of making. From those early days of unknowns to today, as I am approaching ten years of remission, he has been right by my side at every doctor's appointment, treatment, and difficult day I've had. He has also supported me in writing this devotional book, reading and re-reading each devotion and offering suggestions along the way. Norm, I love you and am thankful that you are part of my life!

A special thanks to all my local doctors, nurses, and their staffs, as well as, the Vanderbilt-Ingram Cancer Center Stem Cell Clinic.

INTRODUCTION

None of us can explain the whys of a cancer journey. It just happens. We adjust and learn to deal with it. In the future many may encounter cancer's roadblocks, many already have, some are there now. It's never anyone's choice to be pushed onto the rough cancer route, but a positive attitude far outweighs a negative one when it happens.

Our lives are a journey between our first and last breaths. We won't always experience smooth, straight roads. Some will be long and winding through hills and valleys; others will have sharp curves and unexpected stretches under construction. Nevertheless, whenever we encounter detours and even stop signs, we can travel on and make the best of it if we choose. We may not be sure which route to take at intersections, but we can trust God to know the way and to take care of us whatever our journey holds. I am convinced that God does not make us travel this journey. He goes with us.

When cancer came into my life, I was like most other cancer patients. I was scared, I didn't know what the future would be like, and I cried! Then I picked myself back up and began the hardest fight of my life. Throughout this journey, I have learned many lessons that I would like to share with you. I hope they cushion some of the rough places on your way and give you courage to fight the greatest fight of your life as well. To get you started, here are ten lessons that acted as guard rails to help keep me from going off the road into the ditch of self-pity and depression.

- **Everything is going to be all right.** This was one of the first lessons that I remember being taught as a young child—then it was repeated over and over regardless of what crisis I was dealing with throughout my life. Everything is going to be all right because God is and has always been in control of my life. Things may not be as I had planned them, but in the long run, they have worked out for the best.
- **Live in the present.** Yesterday is gone and tomorrow has not come so make the most of each day. Enjoy the "good" and endure the "bad."

- **Allow others to do for you when you are not able to do for yourself.** I have always been a person who didn't want to impose on others for things I needed, but during a divorce and again during my cancer journey, I had to humble myself to allow others to do things for me, although I never thought my needs were great enough to ask for prayer. Now I know the most important help you can humbly accept from anyone is their prayers for you.
- **Keep a positive attitude.** It may feel like you are the only person in the world going through a rough time, but always remember to cultivate a positive outlook. It will help keep you and those around you out of the dumps.
- **Look for the beauty that surrounds you.** Years ago, a gentleman at my church shared that a diagnosis of cancer had caused him to become aware of nature in a new way. He began to look at the seasonal changes as if each one might be his last, and he wanted to take them all in while he was still alive. I had not taken time to appreciate God's creation prior to my own cancer diagnosis, so I began to pay attention to the clouds, the sky, the trees, birds, plants on the ground, and all the animals and critters that inhabit wherever I am. It's a sure way to lift your mood.
- **Live Like You Were Dying.** The lyrics written by Tim McGraw remind us to take time to enjoy life more fully. That's especially true if you have a cancer diagnosis. Don't die before your life is over. Fight back. Live your best life. Take time to be with family and friends, travel, and check things off your bucket list. Even add new ones while able!
- **Help others who may be going through difficult times.** Volunteering at a charity or joining a ministry where you can make a difference in others' lives gives you purpose. You can even start your own. You can make phone calls or send cards from home. After I recovered from cancer treatment and a stem cell transplant, as a result of receiving encouraging notes myself, I started a card ministry in our church. Check your community for a variety of opportunities for volunteers.
- **Love those around you and don't be judgmental of them.** This one I have had to work on. So many times, when we don't feel well, we are guilty of looking at others and judging them harshly.

A judgmental attitude doesn't help us and can hurt them. Love, on the other hand, helps us all.

- **Be thankful at all times.** As you go through your cancer journey, be thankful that it was caught when it was; that there are doctors available to help you; that there are chemotherapy and radiation treatments and medications to help with their side effects; and finally, be thankful that you have friends to be with you on your journey. Remember that one day may be difficult, but the next one may be better for you. Spend more time counting your blessings than you do counting your problems. There are so many things to be thankful for, so don't forget to thank God for His creation, including you. I have relied on Philippians 4:6 — *Be anxious for nothing, but in everything by prayer and supplication, **with thanksgiving** (emphasis added), let your requests be made known to God.*

- **Most importantly, seek a close relationship with God.** He did not cause you to have cancer. He is the great physician who is with you every step of the way and beyond. I don't know where I would be today without His love and support. I do know where I will be at journey's end. One day He will say, "It's time for you to come home to live with me for eternity," and I will be ready for that next phase of my life when it comes.

DEVOTIONAL READINGS

POSITIVE ATTITUDE

BEAUTY THAT SURROUNDS YOU

LIVE LIKE YOU WERE DYING

HELP OTHERS

BE THANKFUL

CLOSER RELATIONSHIP

SPECIAL DAYS

CANCER

A CUP OF SUFFERING

MATTHEW 26:39 (NLV) *He went on a little farther and bowed with his face to the ground, praying, "My Father! If it is possible, let this cup of suffering be taken away from me. Yet I want your will to be done, not mine."*

As I look back over the last ten years — my life with cancer — I have learned to appreciate what it has given me, rather than taking things for granted. I have learned that I could not be where I am today without walking with my Lord and Savior. Over ten years ago when I first heard the word "cancer," I cried and was fearful of what lay ahead for me and wondered how long I would live. My husband and I have prayed for "this cup to pass from me" as Jesus did in the Garden of Gethsemane over 2000 years ago. I didn't want to have cancer any more than anyone else. I didn't want to undergo the treatments that I had seen so many other people suffer through, but we ended that prayer as Jesus had with, "Yet, I want Your will to be done, not mine." So, we have traveled this cancer journey, not by ourselves, but with God holding hands with both of us. It is not something we could have traveled without Him there to comfort us and give us both strength to endure the treatments and the anxiety that rears its head every time I go for checkups. I mention both of us since my husband has gone through a lot in his care and support for me. This is not something that only the patient goes through; the caregiver does as well. I have had the finest caregiver one can ask for. He has been God's hands and feet when I needed them the most.

We have been so blessed that my treatments and stem cell transplant have kept me in remission for over ten years. We have learned to appreciate each day as it begins, and to enjoy each other and the things we have been able to do together over these last years. Each day we have tried not to let trivial matters interfere with our joy. I don't know how anyone can take this journey without their faith and without God's grace. This has been my experience and I hope it gives everyone reading this the encouragement to turn to God for help in their journey, if they have not already done so. I praise God the Father, Son, and Holy Spirit for my life and the comfort I have experienced each day since first hearing that word, "cancer."

PRAYER: Father, I give thanks for all You have done for me and pray that others facing difficult times will always turn to You for help in their time of need. You alone are our comforter and healer and are always with us if we open our eyes and hearts and acknowledge You. AMEN.

BECAUSE HE LIVES

JOHN 14:19 (NIV) *"Before long, the world will not see me anymore, but you will see me. Because I live, you also will live."*

Bill Gaither wrote a great song of encouragement in "Because He Lives." It expresses the truth that we can know Jesus lives today. When we sing this song in worship, I am reminded that whatever tomorrow brings, I can face it. Today, I currently am in remission from a blood cancer that I know can't be cured but can be treated. Maybe someday it can be cured as many cancers have been, but that day has not yet come.

As I approach each day, I embrace it with joy to know that Jesus is walking along beside me. There were days early in my diagnosis that He had to carry me. I wonder how those who do not have the assurance that Christ died, rose again from the dead, and lives today, get through the tough times in their lives. I have a choice each day as I awaken whether to be joyful for the day and to look forward to what it holds in store for me, or to pull the covers back up and weep for what was in the past.

One of my inspirations comes from a man in our church who has been dealing with the same cancer I have for over seventeen years. As I look at him and we talk about our mutual journey, I am encouraged. When I was diagnosed over ten years ago, I was told the life expectancy was five to seven years before relapse. Knowing that others are far surpassing these estimates encourages me.

PRAYER: Thank You, Father, for Your Son Jesus Christ who was crucified yet rose from the dead to return back to You. He taught us that because He lives, I also will live. My earthly life may end, but my eternal life will be forever. AMEN.

BENDING BUT NOT BREAKING

ROMANS 5:3-5 (NIV) *And we boast in the hope of the glory of God. Not only so, but we also glory in our sufferings, because we know that suffering produces perseverance; perseverance, character; and character, hope. And hope does not put us to shame, because God's love has been poured out into our hearts through the Holy Spirit, who has been given to us.*

As I look out the windows in my home, a strong wind is howling and blowing. The trees are swaying back and forth, bending but not breaking. Sometimes trees are blown very lightly by a gentle, cooling breeze. There are other times when the wind increases to storm or tornado levels and they bend to the point of breaking, ending up on the ground uprooted or upon our homes or businesses, creating devastation. Their strength has been breached due to internal decay in many instances. Walking through the woods, we often see trees down from high winds and notice the center of the tree has rotted out, leaving it with no strength to withstand high winds. Bugs and insects set up home in these trees causing them to die from the inside out.

Our lives are sometimes no different than these trees when we do not depend upon God in the midst of the storms of life. If we fail to feed our souls with the Word of God, we start dying spiritually from the inside out. No one sees what is going on in our lives until we have been attacked from the inside so severely that the damage seeps through to our outward appearance, changing the way we treat others and how we react to certain circumstances. Then when the storms of life come upon us, we too will become broken, uprooted and infested, like the trees.

If we seek God's guidance, we will be able to bend but not break when the storms of life come our way. We will have the strength of the Holy Spirit to guide and support us if we have fed ourselves with God's Word. When we face loss of jobs and other significant changes in life—cancer and other illnesses, divorce, or even the deaths of family and friends— how we handle these events depends upon our relationship with our Lord and Savior. Will you bend or break when they occur in your life?

PRAYER: Lord, help us to keep our bodies and minds fed with Your Word so that when the strong winds of life come upon us, we will be able to bend but not break. We are being challenged throughout our lives to turn away from You, but we know we will be able to withstand these challenges with Your help. Keep us close. AMEN.

CANCER'S JOURNEY

MATTHEW 26:39 (NLT) *"My Father! If it is possible, let this cup of suffering be taken away from me. Yet I want your will to be done, not mine."*

During our lifetime, many of us will be diagnosed with cancer and will pray the same prayer Jesus did prior to his journey to the cross. ""My Father! If it is possible, let this cup of suffering be taken away from me. Yet, I want Your will to be done, not mine."

Some cancers are minor compared to others with lengthy treatments, surgeries, and ultimately death. Whatever the type of cancer, when someone hears that dreaded "C" word, it is the beginning of a journey that none of us wishes to take. Some people choose to fight it, like I have; others choose to let it take its course. Each one has that choice. There will be good days and bad days, but that is true whether you have cancer or not.

Recently, my book club discussed cancer and its effect on individuals. The question was asked as to whether they would undergo the treatment knowing the side effects and all that their treatment would entail. I am one who chose to undergo treatment and have been in remission for ten years. I know that my cancer is one that cannot be cured, but with the advancements in treatment, I can live longer than if I do nothing. I try not to dwell on the "what-ifs" or the "when" and enjoy every day as it comes.

My mother was diagnosed with colon cancer and breast cancer at the same time and went through treatment for both. She was in remission for nearly a year before having to restart her chemo. She enjoyed every day she had and fought back. We, her children, were able to enjoy our mom for several years that we would not have had with her if she had chosen to not undergo treatment, as difficult as it was at times. I have had several friends who continued with their treatments until they quit working. I can honestly say that none of them ever gave up. They spent more time with their spouses, family, and friends, appreciating every day that God had given them. I also have heard of others who have chosen not to go that route, after seeing family members go through cancer treatments, hoping to spare their families more grief.

PRAYER: God, be with us when we hear "you have cancer." Through Your Holy Spirit, guide and direct us as we make decisions regarding the road ahead in our cancer journey. Be with us in the good days and the difficult ones. AMEN.

DENIAL

1 CORINTHIANS 15:58 (NIV) *Therefore, my dear brothers and sisters, stand firm. Let nothing move you. Always give yourselves fully to the work of the Lord, because you know that your labor in the Lord is not in vain.*

Years before I was diagnosed with cancer, my mother was diagnosed with breast and colon cancer at the same time. She had a colon biopsy revealing cancer. As they prepared her for surgery, suspicious places in her breasts were discovered. My sister and I had traveled to be with her and couldn't believe what we were hearing. When she went to surgery for colon cancer, the doctors biopsied her breasts with the test results coming back positive for cancer in both of them. As a result, she decided to have bilateral breast mastectomies. Two weeks after the breast surgery, she started treatment for both cancers.

Before her surgery, she told me that she had a talk with God and told Him that she was ready for whatever His will was, whether she lived or went to live with Him. She said that she would do whatever God led her to do the remaining days she had left to live. She never complained about losing her breasts, the chemo, or how she felt. Only after her death did my sister and I learn how she lived her last three years. The nurses in the chemo room talked about her as being the cheerleader for everyone receiving their treatments on her day.

I had lost a few friends to cancer prior to my mother's diagnosis, but no one as close. I went into a state of denial. My mother can't die! She's going to beat this terrible disease! I would talk to her nearly daily, but we wouldn't discuss all the side effects she was experiencing. I tried to avoid discussing her treatment and she did as well.

Just as I had done with my mother, so have my children reacted toward me. We talk about everything except my cancer. It has been through their reaction to me that I have realized how I had reacted toward my mother. Cancer is something that we need to discuss with our families when we are going through it. It needs to be brought forward rather than being pushed away. We learn by discussing it. Denial doesn't help anyone, but understanding does, and we gain strength to go on. Through it all, we have someone who is traveling along with us who knows all about denial and understanding: it is our God who holds us in His arms.

PRAYER: Lord, enable us to discuss with family and friends what we are going through when we have been diagnosed with cancer. Don't let us treat the cancer diagnosis as a taboo subject that we avoid mentioning. Let us be open to discuss our fears and pains with those who love us and enable them to be willing to listen to us and support us during trying times. AMEN.

DESERT TIMES

PHILIPPIANS 4:19 (NIV) *And my God will meet all your needs according to the riches of his glory in Christ Jesus.*

Our small study group studied Ray Vander Lann's book *Walking with God in the Desert*. In it, he discusses the desert where the children of God wandered for 40 years and how God provided for them during their desolate years, as well as how God provides for us during our "desert" times.

None of us gets through this life without facing our own personal deserts. At some time, we experience the loss of a loved one, the diagnosis of an illness that changes the way we have been living, or the loss of a job, to mention just a few. The only way to get through our desert times is to turn to God who sustains us. Sometimes we just have to cry out as did Moses, who prayed for God to provide food for the Israelites during those difficult 40 years of wandering in the desert. Our friends, church members, pastors, and family members are ready and willing to intercede for us during our desert times, if we will just ask.

The desert time for each of us may be a lengthy period of time or it may be short lived, but it happens to each of us at some point. God will provide for our every need, whether it is water to drink, food to eat, or a cool tree to provide shade from the intense heat. Just be willing to ask for help when you are faced with a desert in your life. God will provide!

PRAYER: Father, we pray that You will always be there for us whenever we are in desert times. May we be willing to accept help from neighbors and friends when we are faced with desert times and may we provide for others when they are in their deserts. In Jesus name, AMEN.

DOUBT

JOHN 20:29 (NKJV) *Jesus said to him, "Thomas, because you have seen Me, you have believed. Blessed are those who have not seen and yet have believed."*

The disciples were wondering what was going to happen to them that night after they learned that Jesus was not in the tomb, but had risen from the dead. Suddenly, they were faced with the risen Christ and that doubt subsided as He shared with them, and reassured them of their (and our) mission in the world. All were present except Thomas. When he heard of Jesus' appearance, he told the others that he would have to see the holes in Jesus' hands and side to believe. He doubted that Jesus had appeared to them until he saw for himself. When Jesus appeared again with Thomas present, then Thomas saw the wounds and believed.

How many times do we doubt that things are true, have happened, or will happen to us? We as humans are no different from Thomas and we frequently want to "see" for ourselves that things are true. We need to adopt the faith to believe without seeing. During my cancer journey, I have felt a reassurance from God that everything was going to be alright. That positive reassurance is what keeps me going day after day. I know that, one day, cancer will raise its ugly head again and I will be back in treatment again. Eventually I will no longer be able to fight it off and will return to my Heavenly Father. But, in the meantime, I will continue to enjoy life as I am doing now. I believe that life is good and that God is with me every step of the way. The doubt that God has forsaken me is gone away. I know He lives within me guiding every step of my life. Put away the doubt and live the life God has designed for you!

PRAYER: Jesus, keep us in Your care and whenever we feel like being a "Doubting Thomas," show us Your wounds so that we will believe and know that You are right here with us and are caring for us every step of the way. AMEN.

FEAR NOT

ISAIAH 41:10 (NKJV) *"Fear not, for I am with you; Be not dismayed, for I am your God. I will strengthen you, Yes, I will help you, I will uphold you with My righteous right hand."*

Several years ago, I was diagnosed with Multiple Myeloma, a blood cancer. After chemo treatments, a stem-cell transplant and a maintenance regime, I remain in remission. Life had been good and I was enjoying every day I have been given, until last week when a bone study showed I had progression of the disease. I am now awaiting a return to my transplant team at a major medical center. I have known from the beginning that though my cancer is treatable it is not curable; at some point I would relapse. I just wasn't ready to hear this so soon!

Fear of the unknown has once again reared its ugly head. What will I have to do? What will the future hold? Why me? All these questions come into view once again. Upon the initial diagnosis, I experienced these same thoughts and feelings. I know that many others have faced these same fears when faced with a cancer or other debilitating diagnosis, the loss of loved ones, the loss of jobs, or any other crisis. We all at some time will experience events that change the path we have been on, and all we can be assured of is that God is with us every step of the way.

The fear of the unknown can be very stressful. I learned years ago to trust God and He will be with me whatever the future may hold. I have prayed for God to take this away from me, knowing that this cannot be done. Instead, He reassures me that He will be with me whatever circumstances present themselves. I know that He has held me in His arms and comforted me throughout my life. *"Fear not, for I am with you!"*

PRAYER: Father, I give You thanks for being with me each day regardless of the circumstances. I feel Your comforting arms around me when the times are tough. I know that Your will for my life is being accomplished even though it isn't always what I am praying for. For all of this I give You thanks. AMEN.

GIVER OR RECEIVER

LUKE 6:38 (NIV) *Give, and it will be given to you. A good measure, pressed down, shaken together and running over, will be poured into your lap. For with the measure you use, it will be measured to you.*

I was taught from an early age to be a giver, and now I am learning to be a receiver. For those who have been givers most of their lives, this is one of the most difficult lessons to learn. I have cooked meals for friends when they were ill, undergoing cancer treatments, lost loved ones, or I thought they just needed something special to eat. Food is such a healer.

There was a period of time when one of my neighbors had to be out of town at a major medical center during the week for chemo treatments. I would go to their house the day before the trash collector came by, pick up the trash, and carry it to the end of their driveway for pick-up the next morning. I jokingly referred to myself as the trash lady. This is just something you do for neighbors in need. When a need arose, I took friends and neighbors to and from doctor's appointments and children to and from school. But when I needed help, it was difficult for me to ask for it. I was the giver rather than the receiver.

After my cancer diagnosis, it became obvious to me that I had to learn to be a receiver. My husband couldn't do everything for me; I needed outside help. I had avoided asking for prayers when something was going on with me, thinking that my needs were far less than others were. Now when someone asks to pray for or with me, I warmly welcome it. God wants us to learn to be both givers and receivers when the time necessitates it. Jesus gave His life for me and I need to be able to accept that gift, as well as the gifts of others.

PRAYER: Father, help those of us who have spent most of our lives being givers to be able to accept help when we are in need. AMEN.

HELP MY UNBELIEF

MARK 9:24 (NIV) *Immediately the boy's father exclaimed, "I do believe; help me overcome my unbelief!"*

This scripture comes after the disciples had failed to cast out the demon in a young boy. After the father uttered the above statement, Jesus spoke and the demon was cast out. So many times, we, as believers, express the same statement:. "I do believe; help me overcome my unbelief!" How many times have you felt this same way? During my cancer journey, I have gone to Jesus and made the same request numerous times. I know that He can heal me, or at least allow the treatments I undergo to give me a longer and more productive life. My cancer is not curable, but is treatable. With all the progress that has been made in the last ten plus years in the development of new drugs, and means of treatment for those of us with Multiple Myeloma, our lives are being extended every day. Earlier this year CAR-T cell treatment has been approved for relapsed patients which should begin to bring MM closer to a curable cancer. Other cancers have seen great advancements in their treatments, as well. Today, people are living much longer than they were a generation ago.

Even with the advancements in treatment, each of us dealing with cancer still have that doubt and unbelief enter into our minds. How long am I going to live? Can I be cured? What is going to happen next? These questions pop up causing my unbelief to come into being. I know that God is in control of my life, but there are still times when I want to see the results more clearly and have my unbelief wiped away.

PRAYER: Father, so often I am like the father in our scripture who says "I do believe, help me overcome my unbelief." Be with me throughout whatever the future may be. In Jesus name, AMEN.

NAP TIME

MATTHEW 11:28 (NLT) *Then Jesus said, "Come to me, all of you who are weary and carry heavy burdens, and I will give you rest."*

Do you enjoy an afternoon nap? I do, and I have enjoyed one for most of my life! As babies our parents or caregivers fed us in the morning and then would put us down for a nap. Lunch was much the same — eat and nap — and on it goes for months. Ultimately, the baby takes only an afternoon nap. Even after pre-school, kindergarten and then grammar school, naps were part of the day. I remember that after lunch in those early years, we would put our heads down on our desk for a rest before completing our daily work. After I was in college, I would try to schedule my classes with a break between 11:00 and 1:00 and would frequently take a nap during that time.

As life has gone on, I still like a nap. It seems to re-energize me. Many people in the workplace will sit at their desk and take that quick nap after lunch which allows them to refocus for the afternoon. Now that I am retired, I stretch out on my sofa for my nap. During this time, I try to put aside the issues of the day and try to connect with God. I will ask Him to show what He has in store for me. I find that after this time that I am the most creative!

We are not designed to go all day without a rest. When we deal with colds, flu, viruses, cancer, or other illnesses, we need to get plenty of rest so that our bodies can heal. God has told us that if we become weary and heavy laden that we can come to Him and He will give us rest. Take a nap and regenerate!

PRAYER: Help us to recognize that our bodies are not built to be on the run all the time. We need time to rest and let our bodies rejuvenate or heal when we are dealing with an illness, especially cancer treatments, and/or surgeries. AMEN.

NOW WHAT?

ROMANS 8: 38-39 (NKJV) *For I am persuaded that neither death nor life, nor angels nor principalities nor powers, not things present nor things to come, nor height nor depth, nor any other created thing, shall be able to separate us from the love of God which is in Christ Jesus Our Lord.*

In September 2014, I heard the dreaded "C" word. Yes, I had been diagnosed with a blood cancer. The first thought that passed through my mind was "Why me?" I know that many of you have heard that diagnosis as well. I also know that many of you have also experienced the "Why me?" as you have lost loved ones, had heart problems, joint replacements, or other life changing events. But, soon after my diagnosis, I began to think "Why *not* me?" What makes me immune to these life-altering experiences? In such situations our decision then becomes, "What will I do with what has been dealt to me?" I knew that my life was in the hands of God and He would be there to guide me along this journey as He has throughout my life.

Just a few months prior to my diagnosis, I had been at my son's home for a visit and attended their Sunday school class. The lesson that day dealt with a young man who had become a paraplegic and ultimately had begun wheelchair dancing. We were given a card with "Why Me?" on one side; when I turned it over, I found "Now What?" written on the other side. I remembered that card which was in my purse and placed it on my refrigerator as a daily reminder of what I have been asking God ever since. I know that He has things for me to do, and I work hard at staying open to what that soft, sweet voice speaks to me leading me in the direction He has in mind for me. I know one thing for sure, I can't deal with obstacles that come my way without the love and guidance of my Lord and Savior. I also know one other thing, God did not cause me to have cancer, but He has been with me and will continue to be with me on the remainder of my journey.

We were never promised a problem-free life if we believe in Jesus. In fact, we have been told over and over again that we would face trials and tribulations. Jesus is our ultimate example of one who gave His life for each of us. What more horrific way to end life than on a cross? Jesus gave His life so that we can be saved, live life faithfully, and enjoy an eternal life!

PRAYER: I give thanks that You are always with us regardless of what circumstances we may be facing. Also, I know that You do not cause bad things to happen to us, but You will be with us, and all we have to do is accept Your love and support. In Jesus' name I pray. AMEN.

PAINTING THE BARN

PHILIPPIANS 4:6 (NKJV) *Be anxious for nothing, but in everything by prayer and supplication, with thanksgiving, let your requests be made known to God.*

When I was first diagnosed with cancer, my husband and I sat across from the oncologist as he gave us the grave news. After he explained what I would be going through with my treatment, he asked if I had any questions. Hearing all he had to say was far too difficult to take in at that time. The first thing that popped into my head to ask was, "Am I going to lose my hair?" I will never forget his response, "That's like asking what color will we paint the barn when the house is on fire." We all had a laugh! He continued by saying that he had expected me to ask about whether I would live or die.

Sometimes all we can think about in this instance is something as simple as what effect will the chemo have on our appearances. Later on, during my initial treatments, there was an article in a cancer magazine which talked about losing your hair during chemo treatments. It said something like "Don't let your hair determine who you are." I went on through five months of treatments without losing my hair. Next, I underwent a stem-cell transplant where I received strong chemo to kill off everything in my bone marrow before the transplant. Then the day arrived when I had handfuls of hair fall out in the shower. Hair was everywhere, in the bed, on the floor, and on my clothes. I knew that I couldn't save it, so I had my head shaved. I wore little head covers for several months, and then one day, I had the courage to go out in public with my bald head. From that point on, I never wore anything on my head other than the new hairs that were coming in. I will never again complain about a bad hair day. I will never allow my hair to determine who I am.

PRAYER: Our Father, help us to remember it is not our outward appearance that we should be concerned about, but our inward soul which belongs to You. AMEN.

PATIENCE

ACTS1:4-5 (NKJV) *And being assembled together with them, He commanded them not to depart from Jerusalem, but to wait for the Promise of the Father, "which," He said, "you have heard from Me; for John truly baptized with water, but you shall be baptized with the Holy Spirit not many days from now."*

How often have you said, "God, give me patience, and I need it now"? What an oxymoron! We live in an instant-gratification world. When we want something, we go out and purchase it whether or not we have the money or really need it.

As I grew up, I learned be patient and to wait for birthdays and Christmases for my special gifts. Today's children have learned that if they want something their parents, or grandparents, will get it for them. How many times have you been in a store where a child picks up a toy and tells their parent that they want it? The parent tells them to put it back, but the child pitches a tantrum for the toy. And the parent gives in. What is this teaching the child? Is it teaching them to be patient and that at the right time they may receive it as a gift? No! It is teaching them that they don't have to wait for things they want. This is not a good lesson for children no matter their age or circumstances. We learn patience by learning to wait.

As we grow older, lack of learning to be patient and to wait can carry over into our daily lives. We get upset when we go to the grocery and get in a line where the customer takes a long time to check out; we fret when we go to the doctor and have to wait even though we were on time for our appointment; we get upset when we have a dire medical issue that causes us to have to wait for treatment; and we get upset when the traffic slows and backs up on the highway. You can add many other circumstances that cause us to get impatient. Through my own journey with cancer, I am learning to have more patience. I have learned that many of the circumstances mentioned above aren't worth the anxiety and frustration we generate. And in the end, I can't change those things anyway.

When I think of learning patience, I flash back to the disciples who were told by Jesus that they were to stay in Jerusalem until the Holy Spirit came to them. I wonder what was going through their minds at that time. I doubt that there was a lot of patience in that place waiting for something that they probably didn't understand. I imagine throughout their ministry, they experienced frustration and needed patience just as we do today. This is when our prayers for patience are most needed.

PRAYER: Lord, in this instant gratification world we live in, it is so important for us to learn patience. We know that we can't change the circumstances that we are presented with by getting impatient. We also know that You will make everything right in Your time and that we can't change that, but we can pray for You to give us patience until the time comes for Your will to be done in our lives. AMEN.

PEACE THAT PASSES ALL UNDERSTANDING

PHILIPPIANS 4:7 (NIV) *And the peace of God, which surpasses all understanding, will guard your hearts and your minds in Christ Jesus.*

How hard it is to understand the peace that this scripture describes until you experience it firsthand! Years ago, my mother was diagnosed with cancer. The night before she went into surgery, she told me that she had talked to God about her outcome and that a peace about what the future may hold had come over her. She was at peace about her surgery and wanted me to know this. After the surgery, she went through chemo and was in remission for a couple of years before she was called home to be with our Lord and Savior. I couldn't comprehend how peaceful she was with her future at that time.

A couple of years after my current husband and I had married, he faced open-heart surgery. He prayed about it and told me that he was at peace with whatever the outcome might be. I had lost one husband through divorce and now after only two years of marriage, I was facing losing my precious husband. It was difficult to deal with. But he gave me strength to go on by telling me that he had experienced the same peace that my mom had described.

Still, I did not understand the feeling that they both had described to me. When I was diagnosed with cancer myself, I prayed and prayed and prayed to God to be with me during my journey. Shortly after the diagnosis, I was sitting in worship when I had an overwhelming feeling of peace that whatever the outcome, God would be with me every step of the way.

It is interesting that it took these extreme experiences for all three of us to know the peace that passes all understanding. There is no way to describe it or for others to understand until they experience it. I don't know what tomorrow will bring, but I am sure that God will be with me every step of the way and someday will call me home to be with Him. For today, I am at peace with myself, my family, and my life.

PRAYER: Thank You, God, for providing the peace that passes all understanding. Once we experience it, our lives are never the same. We don't know what the future holds, but with the peace You provide, we can face the future unafraid. AMEN.

PRAYER

Throughout my struggles with cancer and other crises in my life, I have learned that the only way I can handle the circumstances is to go to God in prayer and to turn to the scriptures for support. I used to just pray, "God help me. Make things right." As I have grown older and dealt with more important crises, I have learned that my will and God's will may not always be the same. I have also learned that I need to accept that fact, and not give up on my faith, because whatever God's will is during my trying times, He is going to walk hand in hand with me through the difficulty.

I have known many people who faced hardship and believed that God deserted them so they deserted Him. They blamed God for what happened rather than waiting to see how He was working in their lives. On the other hand, many of others faced divorce, lost loved ones, lost jobs, or were diagnosed with cancer and other debilitating diseases, yet continued to rely on God's grace and the redeeming love He has for each one of us.

From the initial diagnosis to the present, I have had support from my friends and family. My faith has not faltered, but grows stronger every day I live. Today is all I have been promised and I will enjoy it and give thanks continually for all the blessings that God has bestowed upon me and my family!

PRAYER: May we continue to stay in constant contact with You through our prayers and as we study Your Word and listen for Your guidance. We are thankful that we have a loving God who cares for us. AMEN.

RACE FOR THE CURE

ISAIAH 40:31(NIV) *But those who hope in the Lord will renew their strength. They will soar on wings like eagles; they will run and not grow weary, they will walk and not be faint.*

Every year the American Cancer Society has a fund-raiser called Race for the Cure. Cancer survivors are invited to walk a designated route to raise money for cancer research. The first year after my stem-cell transplant, I didn't walk. I didn't want to go out with the other cancer survivors because I didn't consider myself a survivor. The following year, my husband and I walked around a track at the fairgrounds. I received my survivor's t-shirt and proudly wore it. My husband walked with me as a caregiver. There were booths around the track with food vendors and other items for sale. As we started walking, the vendors and the people who had come to the event bordered the track, cheering all of us along. Tears began to flow! I have walked every year since, except 2020 when the walk was cancelled due to COVID-19. I look forward to being able to walk again when it is safe.

Our local hospital sponsors a brunch for cancer survivors. It started in the hospital conference room, but quickly moved to the community conference room. Survivors are celebrated at the brunch. There are some who have been survivors for 30 years. It's interesting to see people that I never knew had cancer. I'm always glad to see long-time survivors. They are such an inspiration for me. I know that their cancers are different from mine, but there is always hope for anyone who has received the diagnosis. Hope is what keeps us going.

PRAYER: I pray for Your guidance as we cancer survivors continue to have hope and live a life pleasing to You. Some have been told that they are cured while others are still in the treatment phase or remission, but haven't reached the point where the doctors can say they are cured. Be with each of us as we travel this journey together. We ask this in the name of Your Son, Jesus Christ. AMEN.

WAITING FOR ME
TO COME HOME

MATTHEW 25:13 (NIV) *Therefore keep watch, because you do not know the day or the hour.*

After a dramatic change in my life—divorce in my forties—I went back to school and received my law degree. I worked during the day and went to school at night, so I usually didn't get home until late. I had three kitties waiting for me to come home. When they heard the garage door open, all three came running to the back door, meowing for me. I could hear them before I opened door and went into the house, then they were all over me. Frequently, I stayed up late to organize notes from my classes. One got on the back of my chair and wrapped herself around my neck; another climbed into my lap; and the third curled up in another chair in my office. When I went to bed, each had their spot on the bed up next to me. I felt comforted by my little kitty friends.

That's how I feel with God's arms wrapped around me each day. I know He is waiting for me to come home to be with Him, just like my pets were years ago. He alone knows when I will go home. When the time comes, I will embrace it, knowing I will be welcomed into God's arms!

I'm not saying I want to leave this earthly life today. I hope to live long enough to see my grandchildren marry and have families; I want their children to know their great grandmother. I hope my cancer stays in remission long enough for me to enjoy the dreams I have for the future, but none of that is within my control. God is waiting for the right time for me to come home to Him. However, many people think they may have done things they don't believe God will forgive, even if they ask Him. They fear dying, but He is waiting for them also with welcoming arms.

PRAYER: Lord, be with each of us as we continue our journey here on earth. Draw those who are afraid closer to You and welcome each of us home at journey's end. AMEN.

EVERYTHING WILL BE ALL RIGHT

EVERYTHING WILL
BE ALRIGHT

DEUTERONOMY 31:8 (NIV) *The Lord himself goes before you and will be with you; he will never leave you nor forsake you. Do not be afraid; do not be discouraged.*

My mother came from a generation which didn't talk about their medical problems, politics, or religion. She was always reminding me "everything will be all right" regardless of what was happening. There was a time when I was in college that I didn't find out my daddy had had surgery until I came home for the weekend. She didn't want to upset me during my exams. There were other such examples of not wanting to upset her children with their problems. That's just the way my mother was.

As she went through her cancer treatments, she never complained. We learned at her funeral that she was on one of the cooking teams at her church and throughout her treatments, she would go to the church, cook, but not eat because she was too sick from the chemo. Then there were times when she had meetings that her ride would come to pick her up and she would say to go on because she wasn't able to make it—still never complaining.

As she moved into the final weeks of her life, she was hospitalized and given medications to ease the pain. I was fortunate enough to be able to be with her that last week. She was in a room with two beds and I stayed with her in the second bed. She rarely complained to the nurses, but we could tell when she was suffering and the medical staff was so helpful to put her at ease. Still neither of us discussed her cancer. She would just say, "everything is going to be all right." My two sons were able to get away and come visit her and I'm sure that is what kept her going that last week. After my younger son left, it was as if she had finished her work here on earth. His parting words to her were, "Nana, don't worry, I will take care of Momma." The next day as her nurses, doctor, and I stood by her bedside, she took her last breath. Her work here was over, and she knew "everything would be all right."

This is a lesson a long time coming, but I have finally learned that "everything *will* be all right" if I just keep my eyes on Jesus.

PRAYER: Thank You, God, for letting us know that everything will be all right if we learn to lean on You and trust You. It may not always be what we were looking for or planning for, but with You at our side it is all right whatever the outcome. AMEN.

GREAT IS THY FAITHFULNESS

LAMENTATIONS 3:23 (NLT) *Great is his faithfulness; his mercies begin afresh each morning.*

God told Abraham to take his son Isaac and sacrifice him as a burnt offering. Abraham loved Isaac, but as the scriptures tell us, he did not hesitate in doing what God told him to do. He loaded his donkey with wood for the offering. Somewhere along the way Isaac questioned his father about the lamb for the sacrifice. Abraham told him that God would provide. When they arrived, Abraham did as God had directed and bound Isaac on the altar. As he lifted his arm, knife in hand, an angel appeared and told Abraham that God knew he feared him and would follow his directions. There appeared a ram in the thicket, and Abraham took the ram and offered it as a sacrifice, sparing his beloved son Isaac.

In this story, we see that Abraham exhibited trust in God and feared him so that he was willing even to sacrifice his son. God rewarded Abraham for his obedience, and exhibited His faithfulness by providing the ram for the sacrifice.

I wonder what Abraham was thinking as he followed God's command to offer Isaac on that altar. Abraham showed utmost trust in the faithfulness of God in his response. What would we think in his circumstances? We don't have to go to the lengths Abraham did. We aren't asked to make a sacrifice of anything but our reluctance to trust Him.

PRAYER: God, give us the willingness to follow Your directions in our lives even though we have doubts about the outcomes. May we be faithful in what You call us to do and to be. AMEN.

IN GOD'S ARMS

ISAIAH 46:4 (NLT) *I will be your God throughout your lifetime— until your hair is white with age. I made you, and I will care for you. I will carry you along and save you.*

I had to have back surgery to ease the pain I had endured for the better part of a year. I had tried physical therapy, injections, and medications, all to no avail. Finally, I went to a neurosurgeon who reviewed my tests and history. He told me the only resolution to my problem was surgery. I had heard of terrible outcomes from back surgery and was not that excited about it. I asked God for direction and when the surgeon gave me his opinion, I asked, "How soon can you do it?" I felt confidence in him and the procedure after asking for God's guidance. Surgery was scheduled.

While in the pre-surgery room, I lay on the bed with my mind focused on God's caring for me. I felt arms reaching under my body, lifting me up from the bed, cradling me up close. Then I heard God say to me, "Don't be afraid, everything is going to be all right." Those were the same words I had heard my mother telling me many times during her life. How reassuring they are to this day! After being cradled in God's arms, I was placed back on the bed. I have never before had an experience like this, but I can assure you, I felt like I had an "out of body experience," of being lifted from that bed and held in God's arms for those brief moments.

My husband was the only person in the room with me. When I told him about it tears ran down my face. I knew from that point that I need not worry about the surgery. When I woke up, the pain was gone and continues to be gone. God had used the hands of the surgical team to correct the problem in my back and for that I am so grateful! I know that God is taking care of me just as He does with all who believe in Him.

PRAYER: Lord, when we are worried about health issues and others things as well, we know that You are always there with us. Feeling Your presence is so reassuring and lets us know that You are never more than a prayer away. AMEN.

MIGHTY OAK

JEREMIAH 17:8 (NIV) *They will be like a tree planted by the water that sends out its roots by the stream. It does not fear when heat comes; its leaves are always green. It has no worries in a year of drought and never fails to bear fruit."*

In my backyard are several different species of oak trees. The oak tree is the oldest tree in the eastern part of North America. Its usual life span is 1000 years and they do not produce acorns until they are about 50 years old. In its life span an oak tree can produce over 10 million acorns. The oak tree serves as shade for the area underneath it, food for birds and many ground critters, as well as building material for homes, ships and other structures. God saw a vast list of things that the oak tree can be used for while reproducing itself. It is said that the oak tree has been on the earth over 65 million years. This is primarily due to the hard shell the seed exists in. These were some facts about the mighty oak that I found fascinating.

The oak tree inspires us to be strong and to never give up. We look at the tiny oak seed and then at the giant oat tree and see that many times great things come from tiny beginnings. We can look at so many inventions that have made life easier for us all. I can't imagine how my grandparents and their parents lived without the many conveniences of life we enjoy today! Many of these inventions were mere ideas in one man or woman's mind, but, as the tiny oak seed, they grew to become something remarkable that has made life more enjoyable for all of us — from farming equipment to a better means of keeping warm or cool regardless of the weather. We have vaccines for so many diseases that were not available to prior generations and more are continuing to be developed, thus making life more enjoyable and last longer. Some of these inventions took many years to develop, but those working on them were persistent and never gave up. New cancer treatments and means of detecting cancer earlier are available today that weren't available several years ago. Maybe someday cancer can be wiped out if the researchers keep persistently working on new means of diagnosis and treatment.

As the old saying goes, "Life is tough, but the tough keep going." This is something that we should take away from looking at the mighty oak, which in many cases, is hundreds of years old. It has withstood storms, drought, disease, and other conditions that could have killed it, but it still stands tall as a symbol of how we should live — strong and resilient — regardless of what troubles come our way.

PRAYER: Lord, I pray that You help each of us to be strong and resilient when we are faced with difficult times, using the mighty oak as an example for us. No matter what we are facing, with You by our side we can endure whatever comes our way. In Jesus name, AMEN.

MIRACLES

JOHN 2:11 (NIV) *What Jesus did here in Cana of Galilee was the first of the signs through which he revealed his glory; and his disciples believed in him.*

Do miracles happen today? Throughout the gospels, we read of the miracles that Jesus preformed for those around Him. He turned water into wine, healed the sick, cast out demons, and raised Lazarus from the dead, to mention a few. Some would say that these are only stories from biblical days during Jesus' lifetime.

Think about how many times you hear of miraculous happenings where people were healed when the doctors gave no hope, or accidents where people "should" have been killed, but walked away unscathed. Jesus is still among us, healing and protecting us.

I remember a song about Jesus being a co-pilot. As I have traveled alone from place to place, I try to keep the front passenger seat of my car empty as a reminder that Jesus is with me along the way. I know that I can't see Him and that He is not physically with me, but I do know that His spirit is always there protecting me on my journeys.

We may ask why certain things happened the way they did and why Jesus didn't answer prayers for healing or protection. Why didn't He preform a miracle then? We will never know why things happen the way they do. All I know is that all things happen for a purpose and that God's will will be done on this earth.

Do miracles happen today? Absolutely!

PRAYER: Lord, we don't know why things happen the way they do and we question You with "whys" but we also know that You do not cause bad things to happen to us—sometimes they just happen. The one thing we do know is that You will be with us whatever the circumstances and that miracles do happen when we least expect them. AMEN.

UNANSWERED PRAYERS

---

1 JOHN 5:14 (NKJV) *Now this is the confidence that we have in Him, that if we ask anything according to His will, He hears us.*

How many times have you questioned why God did not answer your prayers the way you wanted them answered, or not at all? Sometimes the answer God gives us is no, or later. We, imperfect and impatient people, want Him to give us what we want when we ask for it. God doesn't work that way. Our time schedule is not the same as His. Who knows, He may have something far greater in store for us than what we think we need!

Years ago, when my former husband left me, I begged and pleaded with God to make him come back, not only for my sake, but for the sake of our children. I cried out to God asking "Why?" to no avail. After my divorce, I moved back to my home state and met a fine man; we've now been married twenty-five years. As I look back, I realize that God had something far better in store for me than what I thought I wanted and needed all those years ago. What do I say now? "Thank You, God for bringing me to the place I am today and with the man I love so dearly!" In retrospect, this is by far a healthier relationship than I previously had. At the time, I couldn't see the big picture that I see today. I now realize that I wasn't praying that God's will be done in my life, but for my will to be done!

Another instance was when a friend's husband was in a private plane crash that left him paralyzed and on a respirator. She prayed continually for him to live. Finally, one of her friends asked her if her prayers were answered and he was allowed to live could she accept his condition? Ever since, I have thought of that question when praying for certain outcomes. We are not to question the whys of God's plans for us. Sometimes unanswered prayer is the best thing for us because it causes us to step back and let God lead us where he wants us to go.

PRAYER: God, help us to understand why You don't answer our prayers in the manner we desire. Help us to accept the fact that You sometimes have better plans for us than we can see or imagine at the time. AMEN.

LIVING IN
THE PRESENT

ENJOY EVERY DAY GOD HAS GIVEN YOU

PSALM 118:24 (NKJV) *This is the day that the LORD has made; We will rejoice and be glad in it.*

Recently, I heard a profound statement: "If you spend too much time thinking about the future, the present will slip through your fingers." How often do we spend so much time thinking about and planning for the future that we fail to enjoy the present? We are given only today, and we should live it and enjoy it for we don't know what tomorrow will bring.

As children we longed for Christmas, our birthdays, summer vacations, and other coming events. It seemed like these would take forever to arrive, but we still longed for them, imagining what we would receive as gifts or where we would go on vacation — always thinking and planning for the future. As we grew older, we longed to reach high school, to graduate, to go to college, to get a job, get married, have children, and have a dream home and friends. I wonder if all the longing kept us from enjoying the present.

As I look back over my life, there were many times that I failed to stop and revel in the moment. How often do you think, "If only I had taken more time doing this or that?" We can never reach back and recover the past and what we may have missed because we were focused too much on the future.

As I grow older, I am reminded to enjoy every day and the joy it brings. The older we get, the more we realize that our tomorrows are fewer and fewer. As a cancer survivor, this is an important part of my everyday life. I know that someday I won't be here. I already know what my future holds. I look forward to resting in peace in my heavenly home with my Lord and Savior.

PRAYER: Lord, help us to enjoy each day You have given us and not dwell on what could have been, or may be, but enjoy what is. We pray this in Jesus' precious name. AMEN.

LIVING IN THE PRESENT

ISAIAH 43:18 (NIV) *Forget the former things; do not dwell on the past.*

MATTHEW 6:34 (NIV) *Therefore do not worry about tomorrow, for tomorrow will worry about itself. Each day has enough trouble of its own.*

Many times, we tend to focus on what has happened in the past, worrying about what we did or didn't do rather than putting the past behind us. It is over—-gone; it won't come back. If we have regrets about what we may have said or done to a family member or friend, it is good to go to him or her and ask for forgiveness. If that is impossible, we can go to our Heavenly Father and ask for forgiveness. He is always waiting for us to come to Him.

I have heard of people lying on their deathbeds, unwilling to give up their earthly life because of something they said or did, or that was said or done to them, by a family member or close friend. They had unfinished business that was keeping them from going on to their eternal home. In many cases, they are relieved when they come face to face with the estranged person and make amends. What a difference this would have made had they chosen to make those amends years previously!

There are also many people spending their lives worrying about what tomorrow will bring. We don't know that until it happens. "What ifs" can cause us to miss out on the blessings each day brings. There is nothing wrong with planning for the future so long as that does not prevent us from focusing on what today has to offer. In fact, we all need to make provision for our future, both spiritually and financially. We need to make financial plans so that we do not become a financial burden on our families when we reach retirement age, and we need to make spiritual decisions so that we will live eternally with our Heavenly Father.

As for me, I choose to live in the present since I can't change the past other than to make amends with those I may have hurt or who hurt me. I don't know what tomorrow will bring, and I don't want to waste today worrying about something that may never happen. Each day has blessings that I enjoy. I choose to live in the present and in the presence of our Lord and Savior!

PRAYER: Lord, help us stay focused on today and all the joys You have in store for us, rather than worrying about things we can't change or things that are yet to come. Today may not be free of worries, but we know that You are here with us regardless of what's happening to us. AMEN.

SIBLINGS

EPHESIANS 4:32 (NLT) *Instead, be kind to each other, tenderhearted, forgiving one another, just as God through Christ has forgiven you.*

Many of us are blessed with siblings, regardless of the relationship; some are biological and others are adopted, but we are all siblings. Even an only child in a family usually has cousins or close friends who fill the role. As we grow up, we often face sibling rivalries. Then, as we grow older, the rivalries subside and loving relationships develop between them.

In those younger years, sibling rivalry may rear its head often. One child feels that the other is getting more attention or getting to do things that he or she isn't allowed to do. I have two sons who experienced sibling rivalry. The older of the two was much taller than the younger, which caused jealousy. There was always competition between the two, some of which was so subtle that only a parent could see it.

One of my fondest moments came when my younger son mentioned in a toast at his brother's wedding that he had tried to grow into his brother's shoes throughout his life, but he had finally realized that he had his own shoes to fill and that was enough. He had matured so much! I was in tears as he told his story. Many things have happened between the two boys since then, but they are closer than they have ever been and would do anything for each other.

I have a younger sister and brother, and we keep in contact with each other more now than when we were younger. There is a plaque on the wall in my kitchen that says, "My sister and friend." I know that whatever may happen in my life, my brother and sister will be there for me. The sibling relationship is something that we should all nurture.

PRAYER: Bless our siblings as we go through life that they will always be close enough to comfort us in times of trials as the hands and feet of Christ. Keep us from developing sibling rivalries that destroy our relationships. AMEN.

WONDERS OF CREATION

PSALM 139:13-16 (NIV) *For you created my inmost being; you knit me together in my mother's womb. I praise you because I am fearfully and wonderfully made; your works are wonderful; I know that full well. My frame was not hidden from you when I was made in the secret place, when I was woven together in the depths of the earth. Your eyes saw my unformed body; all the days ordained for me were written in your book before one of them came to be.*

The writer of Psalm 139 tells us that God knew us even before we were born. God saw us as that sperm and egg united and continued to multiply and divide with tiny cells differentiating into the parts of the human body. I marvel that a microscopic cell knows how to become a bone, an eye, a heart, or one of the other parts of the human body. Only God can guide and direct this marvelous process from the joining of that tiny sperm and egg, each carrying only one half of the chromosomes that unite to give us the DNA we receive from our mother and our father.

We are not some happenstance of creation. We are fearfully and marvelously made and God has a purpose for our lives. Sometimes the we make or circumstances outside of our control may alter our physical beings. Then God alters our course.

We hear of athletes involved in accidents that leave them without limbs or the use of their limbs, who can no longer pursue their sport. Frequently, these persons are led in a new direction that allows them to help others. They can encourage others because of what they have endured. God takes what seems unredeemable and brings good from it.

As I look at the world, it is hard to imagine how we are so marvelously made and how, when events alter our lives, we are given a new direction in life. Only God can make this happen!

PRAYER: We give thanks for the miracle of our creation. You and You alone, God, can create the persons we are. When things happen in our lives, You are there to redirect us into who You want us to be. For this, may we never cease to be thankful. AMEN.

POSITIVE ATTITUDE

BE STRONG AND COURAGEOUS

JOSHUA 1:9 (NIV) *Have I not commanded you? Be strong and courageous. Do not be afraid; do not be discouraged, for the LORD your God will be with you wherever you go.*

As a young child, I had to have my tonsils removed. I was terrified of the hospital since I had been ill previously and had to be hospitalized for many days. When the nurses came to take me to surgery, all I could do was cry and hang on to my mother and great aunt who were with me. I had my favorite doll with me and my aunt told me I could take her with me to surgery to comfort me. She then walked with me to surgery, while I clutched my doll. She kept telling me, "Be strong and courageous." At that age, I didn't fully understand the meaning of being strong and courageous, but those words have become more meaningful as I have grown older. I know that the doll was removed from me when I was put to sleep, but she was back on my bed when I woke up.

Sometimes we need those encouraging words to be strong and courageous, along with a doll or other physical item with significant meaning to hold onto, when we go through difficult times.

My church women's group has a prayer shawl ministry where members knit or crochet prayer shawls for those going through surgery, chemo treatments, deaths of loved ones, or other crises in their lives. The crocheter or knitter prays over each stitch making the shawls and the members of our group pray over them again when they are finished. These shawls give comfort to the recipients just as my doll did for me those many years ago.

We also have the comfort of our Lord as stated in the scripture above. He is always with us even though we cannot physically touch Him. He is present all the time to encourage us to be strong and courageous no matter what the circumstances may be.

PRAYER: Father, we know that You are with us at all times even though we can't see or touch You, yet we know that You are always there to encourage us to be strong and courageous no matter what the circumstances may be. Sometimes, only through Your encouragement are we able to face each new day. AMEN.

COLORED LENS

ISAIAH 41:10 (NKJV) *'Fear not, for I am with you; Be not dismayed, for I am your God. I will strengthen you, Yes, I will help you, I will uphold you with My righteous right hand.'*

What color lens do you look at life through? The lens you choose determines how you respond to joys and adversities. First, there are those who look at life through a cloudy or dark lens. They see everything as woeful. When they get a diagnosis of cancer or another debilitating disease, they are constantly thinking what's going to happen to me? Am I going to die and when? Their response to everything in life is negative. We usually do not enjoy being around them.

Then there are those who look through rose-colored lens. They see everything as okay. They fail to recognize that there will be bad days mixed in with the good days. When the bad days come, they have a hard time dealing with them.

Finally, there are those who look at life and its circumstances through a clear lens, realizing that in addition to the good days there will be bad days. When the bad days come, when they don't feel like getting up in the mornings, when the side effects of medication become a reality, they are able to accept what is happening and go on with their lives.

It is very easy to slip into either the too negative or the too positive way of looking at life. A clear lens keeps you more stable. You realize that there are going to be bad days, but with a positive attitude of acceptance, you know there are better days ahead and that you won't be alone during those times.

If you look through a dark lens, know that God is with you even when you struggle to see the light at the end of the tunnel. God *is* light and things will look better when you see clearly. Let Him hold you in His arms during the bad days. What a blessing it is to know He is always present!

PRAYER: Lord, help us to look at life and its experiences with a clear lens, knowing that there will be difficult dark days ahead, but also bright and sunny ones as well, knowing throughout all days that You are right there beside us. AMEN.

COMMUNITY

JEREMIAH 29:11 (NIV) *For I know the plans I have for you," declares the Lord, "plans to prosper you and not to harm you, plans to give you hope and a future.*

After my divorce, I quickly learned that you don't fit into couples' groups any more. You become the odd-person-out when friends are planning parties. Thankfully, when I moved back to Tennessee, I was directed to a singles Sunday school class the first time I went to church. It quickly became a community for me and many other singles. We had strong, Biblical lessons and we also enjoyed social events together. I instantly had new friends and a support network. We had monthly potluck dinners and often went out to restaurants together. There were game nights, pool parties in the summer, and many other activities. Classes were even held for divorce recovery and healing.

One of the greatest gifts I received out of that class was meeting my current husband. We got to know each other by attending for several months before he asked me out on a date. From then on, we knew we were meant to be together. That class was exactly what I needed at that time in my life. I know God guided me to that class and those new friends.

PRAYER: Lord, when we open ourselves to Your guidance, we never know where it may lead us. Whether we are facing loss from a divorce, death of a spouse or other loved one, or loss of health due to cancer or other disease, we can always count on You to provide a community of support for us. We give You our thanks, AMEN.

CUB SCOUTS

PROVERBS 22:6 (NKJV) *Train up a child in the way he should go, and when he is old he will not depart from it.*

I volunteered to be a Den Mother when my first son was old enough to join the Cub Scouts. I had no idea what I was doing, but felt called to lead the group of young boys in their scouting experience. Looking back, I feel I gained as much being their Den Mother as they did from being scouts. I planned adventures and experiences for them as well as activities that were necessary for achievement badges. Sometimes they pushed my comfort level—like baiting a fishing hook with worms (they were afraid to touch them) and climbing to the top of a fire tower (I don't like heights). I lead them through Cub Scouts until they graduated to Webelos. I admit there were times when I wondered what I was doing. There were also times my patience was put to the test, with six young boys in second through fourth grades. One day my pastor told me that there must be a special place in heaven for Den Mothers, but I wouldn't trade anything for the experiences we shared. I hope those boys, now in their early 50's, fondly remember being Cubs. I do, and happily, both my sons achieved the rank of Eagle Scouts.

Proverbs 22:6 reminds us to "Train up a child in the way he should go, and when he is old, he will not depart from it." This is our job as parents to our own children as well as those with whom we come in contact. The lack of training children in the way they should go is one of the problems our society faces today.

PRAYER: Father, help parents remember Proverbs 22:6; help them to realize that who we are as adults is dependent upon how we were raised as children. Children are precious to You and need to be treated as such by all of us. Be with each parent reading this devotion and guide them in raising their children. AMEN.

DAMASCUS ROAD EXPERIENCE

ACTS 9:17 (NKJV) *And Ananias went his way and entered the house; and laying his hands on him he said, "Brother Saul, the Lord Jesus, who appeared to you on the road as you came, has sent me that you may receive your sight and be filled with the Holy Spirit."*

One day Saul, a great persecutor of the early Christians, had an encounter with Jesus on the road to Damascus. After this encounter, he became one of the strongest supporters of Jesus and today still has an impact on each of us in our spiritual journey through his Letters in the New Testament. Not many of us have a life-changing experience as Paul did. Many of us were born into a family of believers and were brought up in the church learning of Jesus' love from an early age. Others have a conversion experience at some point in their lives where suddenly their lives are changed as was Paul's.

After Paul's conversion, he spent the remainder of his life preaching and teaching about Christ to everyone who would hear. All we need to do is to believe and accept the forgiving nature of our Lord. This does not mean that after our conversion our lives will be trouble–free, however, we live knowing that Jesus will never leave or forsake us no matter what. Paul was persecuted, imprisoned, and beaten nearly to death, but he did not waver in telling others of Jesus' life, crucifixion, and resurrection. So, it is with us. We are not promised that everything will be easy when we accept Jesus as our Lord and Savior. In fact, Paul tells us in 2 Timothy 3:12 that we will face adversities, but we have the comfort of knowing that we are not alone when these challenges come to us.

PRAYER: Lord, teach us to be strong in our belief in You and the love You have for each of us just as Paul was, regardless of the adversities that may come our way. We know You are always with us, but sometimes we may tend to forget when the difficult times come in our lives. Keep reminding us of Your presence in our lives. AMEN.

DO UNTO OTHERS

MATTHEW 7:12 (NKJV) *Therefore, whatever you want men to do to you, do also to them, for this is the Law and the Prophets.*

Most of us learned the Golden Rule at some time in our early childhood, either in Sunday school or elementary school. "Do unto others as you would have them do unto you." How many times do we think about what we are doing and how it affects others? Most of the time, I try to think how I would feel if they treated me the same way. When I listen to that "still, small voice" within me directing my actions, I feel good about how I treated someone else, but when I fail to listen and do something that hurts another, boy, do I feel bad!

On the other hand, we shouldn't live our lives doing the right things merely in expectation of what someone else would do for us. This is a trap many people fall into. They spend time worrying about what others want them to do rather than doing what God wants. We are marvelously created and unique persons, and we need to be who God created us to be.

PRAYER: Lord, guide our lives so that we are constantly aware of how we treat each other, so we don't knowingly say or do something that hurts others either physically or emotionally. AMEN.

DON'T LET FEAR KEEP YOU FROM BEING HAPPY

ROMANS 8:38-39 (NKJV) *For I am persuaded that neither death nor life, nor angels nor principalities nor powers, nor things present nor things to come, nor height nor depth, nor any other created thing, shall be able to separate us from the love of God which is in Christ Jesus our Lord.*

I recently heard the above scripture and it caused me to stop and think about whether I have allowed fear to keep me from being happy. I also thought of so many others that have failed to do things in their lives due to some kind of fear. There are those who will not go out into public places, travel, or be in a crowd where they feel anxious about escaping due to agoraphobia. Others may fear heights, closed areas, various animals or pets. Their fears prevent them from enjoying the beauties and experiences God created for them. In addition, many fear contracting cancer or other diseases that would change their lifestyle, and many are fearful of dying.

What we do with fear is important. Each of us may react differently when it comes into our lives. We may choose to be hermits in our homes, shutting ourselves off from the outside world, including friends and neighbors. We may choose to be angry about a diagnosis and blame God for our circumstances. Anger produces a mental illness causing further separation from others, affecting our happiness and enjoyment of life. Life is too short to spend it being unhappy or fearful. We can choose to be optimistic. Jesus assures us that He is with us regardless of the circumstances. I often visualize being comforted, wrapped in God's arms, remembering that nothing can separate us from His love and care. I choose to rely on His reassurance.

PRAYER: Lord, thank You for being with us at all times and for taking away fearfulness that prevents us from enjoying the beauty that surrounds us and the happiness You desire for each of us. AMEN.

HONESTY

COLOSSIANS 3:9-10 (NIV) *Do not lie to each other, since you have taken off your old self with its practices and have put on the new self, which is being renewed in knowledge in the image of its Creator.*

Have you heard the saying, "Honesty is the best policy"? Are you always honest with yourself, your family, friends, work colleagues, and others? Very few, if any, can answer in the affirmative. More important, "Are you honest with God?" We can hide lies we tell others, but God knows our heart and He knows when we are being dishonest with Him.

Throughout the Bible there are examples of people being confronted by God about their behaviors (and they thought that they could get away with what they had done)! Some ran and hid as Adam and Eve, Jacob just lied to his father in order to take his brother Esau's birthright. They did it and we're still doing it. Deceit is everywhere and we continue to see it daily in our own lives and on the news. When we get caught, do we always admit to what we have done or do we lie about it? What happens next? We continue to tell lies to cover up the prior lies until we can't remember what we did in the first place. Being honest, regardless of the outcome, is so much easier. The solution is to put on the new self made possible by God.

PRAYER: Lord, help us to put away the old self and concentrate on being a new person learning to be truthful to ourselves and with You. AMEN.

LET GO AND LET GOD

MATTHEW 28:20 (NKJV) ... *lo, I am with you always, even to the end of the age.*

Most of us have faced times in our life when we wonder how we will get from one day to the next, even from one breath to the next. There was a time in my life when I thought I had it all. Life was good! Then one day I woke up and things had changed; my life would never be what it had been. My husband of 17 years and the father of our two teenaged sons had chosen to leave me. Through those days I realized, probably for the first time in my life, how much I needed God in all aspects of my life and how much I depended upon Him in order to go on. I realized that God places angels along our path to minister to us in time of need. I had friends who had been peripheral friends but who in this situation became close intimate friends. There were people I would never have met in my previous circumstances.

One friend invited me to go on a "Walk to Emmaus," a three-day spiritual retreat, which was a major mountain-top experience for me. I learned the joy of true Christian friendship through the Walk and in the days and years that followed. I learned to open myself up to others and talk about my hurts and joys with my Christian friends, along with learning about their hurts and joys. I was born into a Christian family and had been involved in my church wherever I had lived, but I had not grown as a Christian like I have since this chain of events took place. I learned that I could not handle life's challenges on my own. How often we all fall into the hole of believing we can! Only when I was at my lowest point did I decide to look UP and see who had been taking care of me all along. I had to let go of a lot of things and turn them all over to God. What a blessing that has been to me! God is not always gentle in His nudging; sometimes He has to hit us on the head to get our attention!

When we are faced with life-changing events, we each need to remember God is always with us. We need to open our eyes and see Him, open our ears and hear Him, and follow His leading. Jesus reminds the disciples in the Great Commission, *".... lo, I am with you always, even to the end of the age."*

PRAYER: Lord, no matter what crisis we may be facing today, whether it be divorce, health issues, loss of a job, or whatever else we may be facing in our lives, remind us that You are with us at all times. We do not have to face these times alone. AMEN.

RAINBOWS

GENESIS 9:12-16 (NIV) And *God said, "This is the sign of the covenant I am making between me and you and every living creature with you, a covenant for all generations to come: I have set my rainbow in the clouds, and it will be the sign of the covenant between me and the earth. Whenever I bring clouds over the earth and the rainbow appears in the clouds, I will remember my covenant between me and you and all living creatures of every kind. Never again will the waters become a flood to destroy all life. Whenever the rainbow appears in the clouds, I will see it and remember the everlasting covenant between God and all living creatures of every kind on the earth."*

I love to look for a rainbow after a storm. I have seen them anywhere from faint "bows" to bright colors, single "bows" to double ones, and one time there was a triple one! Years ago, after a morning of intense rain with almost constant thunder, I remember walking out of our church to the sight of a bright double rainbow in the calm sky. As we left the worship service inside, awe and worship continued outside the sanctuary.

I also remember driving down the road after a storm, finding a rainbow ahead of us, and following it as we drove. The end of the rainbow was coming to the ground and as we got closer, we could see the reflection of the colors on the white siding of a building. The sign in front of the building was "Rainbow Daycare." How appropriate!

God set the rainbow in the sky after the Great Flood, as a sign that He would never destroy the world with water again. I feel as Noah's family would have. Full of hope. They had hope for a new future. The rainbow reminds me of the promise God made to Noah and his family, but it also reminds me of hope for a better day when I go through the storms in my life: trying times with children or parents, deaths of loved ones, loss of a job or source of income, illnesses such as cancer, or some other debilitating disease or accident resulting in loss of mobility or activity in one's life. We all go through some of these storms throughout our lives, but God continues to send us rainbows of hope for a better tomorrow. That better tomorrow may come here on earth or may be lived out in eternity with God. When it comes, it results in a promise from God that the storm will not last forever, there are better days ahead, just as he did with Noah and his family.

PRAYER: May we always look for a rainbow at the end of a storm and have hope for a better day ahead. You promised Noah and his family that You would never destroy the world with a great flood, and You promised us that You would be with us no matter what storms we may be facing in life. For this, we give thanks every day. AMEN.

SHE WATCHES FROM ABOVE

JOHN 14:16 (NKJV) *And I will pray the Father, and He will give you another Helper, that He may abide with you forever.*

On the first anniversary of my mother's death, I was having a difficult day. As I pulled into the parking lot at my office, I opened the car door and a white feather flew into the car. I tried to catch it, but it was too elusive. After a minute or two it flew out the door, just as it had come in. At that moment, I felt peace and comfort that I can only explain as being from our Heavenly Father.

At this time, one of my favorite TV shows was *Touched by An Angel*. At the close of each show, a white feather floated across the screen. As this feather came into my car and then exited, I felt that it was a sign from above that my mother was still watching over me and giving me the comfort that I needed that day and at that time. Today when I see a feather floating around me, I am reminded that my mother is still looking after me from her heavenly home.

When Jesus was ascending to His Father and leaving his disciples, they were worried and concerned about what they were going to do without their friend and teacher. Jesus assured them that a Comforter would be sent to them in the form of the Holy Spirit. We all have that Comforter in our lives if we are willing to accept Him. Sometimes we need a visual to reassure us that we are being cared for and looked after. The feather was the visual I needed that day.

PRAYER: Thank You, God, for providing visual reassurances of Your presence in our lives that remind us that You are always with us. In Jesus name, we pray. AMEN.

WHO AM I?

PSALM 139:13-14 (NIV) *For you created my inmost being; you knit me together in my mother's womb. I praise you because I am fearfully and wonderfully made; your works are wonderful, I know that full well.*

Do you ever wonder who you are? When we are born, we are known as our mother and father's child, or the grandchild of our grandparents. Then when we get married, we become someone's spouse. After we have children, we become our child's mother or father, and then the child's grandparents. We are sisters or brothers to our siblings. Do you get the idea how we are associated with other members of the family?

The most important relation any of us can have is as a child of God. He is the one who made us and sustains us. I read Psalm 139 and marvel at God's creations, not only what we see around us every day, but at His creation of ME! He knew me when I was first conceived! He put my parts together in the womb and then He continues to mold me into the marvelous creation I am today, and you as well. That is inconceivable in my finite mind, as I am sure it is to you. Our responsibility is to live according to the desires of our Heavenly Father.

Every day we see those who may be considered "imperfect" in the world's eyes, but in God's eyes, there are no imperfect people. I think of the many accomplishments of others who may not see, hear, be able to walk, or do other things that we are able to do and take advantage of. They did not give up, nor did their parents, when the times were tough. They persevered to become the marvelous persons God intended them to be.

Who am I? I am a marvelous child of God! With all the imperfections I may have, God uses me to perfect his kingdom here on earth.

PRAYER: May we never forget that we are treasured children, created by You, our Heavenly Father. Thank You for loving me regardless of any imperfections I may have now. AMEN.

WOE v. JOY

1 THESSALONIANS 5:16-18 (NIV) *Rejoice always, pray continually, give thanks in all circumstances; for this is God's will for you in Christ Jesus.*

Years ago, a TV game show's contestants chose doors to open. Behind one door was a big prize. Similarly, in our lives we also have doors to choose between. There is the "Woe-is-Me" door or the "Joy" door.

The "Woe is Me" door, unfortunately, is the door many choose to open. All they can think of is that they don't have what others may have such as jobs, education, health, good looks, athletic prowess, homes, cars, or something else. Many of these things are material. Woe-is-me people are continually looking at what others have that they want rather than rejoicing in what they already have. Someone out there will always have less or more than we have. We close the woe-is-me door when we choose to be thankful for what we have rather than what we don't have. We can go through the woe-is-me door and be unhappy. We may end up depressed if we focus on the negative rather than the positive in life.

The other choice is the "Joy" door. When we go through this door, we choose to find joy in what we have rather than what we don't have. First and foremost, we have our health, whatever it may be; we have our families, wherever they may be; we have our friends; and most of all we have the promise of eternal life through Jesus Christ. People who are thankful for all they have, live life abundantly. Many of these people may endure limitations or health issues that prohibit them from enjoying what they may have had in the past, but they are still joyful and express that joy to all with whom they come in contact.

Which door do you choose to open? As for me, I choose the door to gratitude and joy, and I hope to share that joy with all whose path I cross.

PRAYER: Help us to choose to be joyful and thankful rather than feeling sorry for ourselves when adversities come our way. Remind us that You are always with us to guide and walk with us when difficult times occur. AMEN.

BEAUTY THAT SURROUNDS YOU

BEAUTY OF CREATION

JOB 12:7-10 (NIV) *But ask the animals, and they will teach you, or the birds in the sky, and they will tell you; or speak to the earth, and it will teach you, or let the fish in the sea inform you. Which of all these does not know that the hand of the LORD has done this? In his hand is the life of every creature and the breath of all mankind.*

D o you take time out of your busy day to notice all the creatures and plants and trees that God has placed here on this Earth? I admit there have been times in my life that I was so busy running a household, raising children, volunteering, then going back to work after my children were grown, that I failed to take time to look around at God's gifts to us. After retirement, I have more time to sit and marvel at all the living things that are around me and also to notice the formations of rocks and mountains, especially in the part of the country in which we live. Sometimes I even take time to chuckle at some of these. God must have had fun creating all the marvels of this world!

We may travel far and wide to see some of these creations from the majestic snow-covered mountains of Alaska, to the Grand Canyon, various National Parks, the beauty of the calm seas and then the wild and dangerous seas, many waterfalls from Niagara Falls to the smaller ones, yet the beauty of creation is around us all the time if we just stop and look and listen.

I have learned that I can walk in my own backyard, hike the many trails in our community, or just sit and look out at nature from my deck and marvel at creation. I realize I have so much beauty right before me that I frequently fail to notice. I watch the tiny hummingbirds to the large turkey vultures fly around. A turkey flock wanders through our area occasionally and on one of their trips we saw thirty-two turkeys, from small baby ones to the large toms. Deer wander through the woods, sometimes eating many of our plants, but they still are a joy to watch. This year we have had a lot of rain and the moss on the large rocks in our backyard is very deep and plentiful along with the lichens on the rocks and trees. Wildflowers blooming throughout the year are also a joy to see.

God made all these things and He made them for our enjoyment. We need to take time to notice and listen to the marvels of nature as we get away from our busy life and give thanks to God for His majestic creations.

PRAYER: Thank You, God for the beauty of Your creation. May we all take time out of our busy lives to stop and enjoy our surroundings and give thanks for that beauty which You have created. AMEN.

CHAOS

GENESIS 1:1-2 (NKJV) *In the beginning God created the heavens and the earth. The earth was without form, and void; and darkness was on the face of the deep.*

Years ago, during a Bible study when our former pastor was teaching on Genesis, he started at the beginning of creation with the world being a mass of chaos. Being a visual person myself, I can imagine God taking the mass of chaos and molding it into the heavens and earth. He then spoke the words "Let there be light" and there was light. He went on to create the heavens and earth as we know it today and ultimately, He created man. Everything was in a sequential order—well planned out. Man could not have created what we have today. Only God who has been, is, and will always be, could have done this!

Our pastor went on to say that chaos still exists today in the lives of mankind and we need to turn our cares and worries over to God for Him to make something beautiful out of our chaos. At that time, my husband and I were trying to sell our former home and move where we live today. This was not the best time to be selling real estate considering the financial crisis of 2008-2009. It just happened to be the time we had planned to retire, build our retirement home, and settle down into a simpler way of life. Our house had been on the market for two years at this time and prices had dropped dramatically.

After the study, we were invited to the chancel rail to pray and turn our cares (and chaos) over to God. We did and while we were still at the church, we had a call for a showing of our house the next day. We had the house in pristine condition and went to lunch while it was being shown. We prayed for God's will to be done. The next day we had an offer and negotiated the details to a point we could accept. From then on, our current life began as we had dreamed it would. It took us just asking God to take our chaos and turn it into something special He had planned for us. God created in the beginning, and continues to create excellent outcomes if we just have faith and let His will be done in our lives.

PRAYER: God, we know that You are the great creator of all things. You took chaos and made something beautiful out of it. Help us to always turn to You when we are faced with uncertainty and look for Your guidance in our lives. Only You can make something beautiful out of the chaos we face every day. AMEN.

DIAMOND IN THE ROUGH

EPHESIANS 4:11-12 (KJV) *And he gave some, apostles; and some, prophets; and some, evangelists; and some, pastors and teachers; For the perfecting of the saints, for the work of the ministry, for edifying of the body of Christ.*

It is amazing at how diamond cutters can take a raw diamond and turn it into what we see and admire as a sparkling diamond set into a ring, pendant, other piece of jewelry, or in a work of art. No one would want to use a raw diamond for a ring! But its beauty is revealed when the master cutter finishes with it; then it is desired all over the world.

Perfectly cut, a diamond reflects the colors of the prism as it reacts to the light coming into it. So are we when we have turned our lives over to the master diamond cutter, Jesus. He takes us as He finds us and woos us to Him. As we accept Jesus as our Lord and Savior, He begins to mold us into a beautiful diamond that reflects His life in us. We are a new creation — a sparkling diamond! Just as the diamond cutter can't be too fast in working with the raw stone or he will destroy the beauty that lies within it, so does Jesus work with us in our lives. The cutter takes the raw stone, studies it, measures it, and looks for the reflections of light to create a finished product that will be desirable to one seeking the stone.

Raw diamonds have different qualities with some being more brilliant than others, or some whiter or clearer than others. The master diamond cutter still works with the raw stone. Some are not the quality for jewelry and end up in the industrial market. In other words, there are places for all kinds of diamonds. So, it is with us. In God's eyes, we all have a place in His Kingdom. No job is insignificant in God's eyes so long as we follow His leadership in our daily lives. We don't know what God has in store for us. We must be willing to study, listen and follow wherever He leads, remembering He and He alone has plans far beyond what we could ever imagine on our own!

PRAYER: Each of us is like a raw diamond until You take control of our lives and give us Your gifts. Some of us are chosen for leaders and others for workers, but each job is especially designed for the particular person and is part of Your overall plan. Everybody can't be a leader — some have to be workers and vice versa. We all have a place in Your world. Thanks be to God! AMEN.

DO NOT PUT YOUR LIGHT UNDER A BASKET

MATTHEW 5:15-16 (NKJV) *Nor does anyone light a lamp and put it under a basket, but on the lampstand, and it gives light to all who are in the house. Let your light shine before men in such a way that they may see your good works, and glorify your Father who is in heaven.*

Looking back at early days of civilization, people had to rely upon the sun during the day for light and the moon for light at night. They studied the stars to assist them in their travels at night. As man developed, he learned to have fires both to keep warm and to light the night. Moving forward, man learned to have oil lamps to light the night and then candles. Today with the advent of electricity, we move freely throughout our homes with the flip of a light switch whether it is the middle of day or the middle of the night. We have a manmade source of light at all times wherever we may be.

Where we lived several years ago, people in some neighborhoods would put luminaries out to line the streets the second Saturday night during the Christmas holiday season. Carloads of people would drive through the neighborhoods to view the Christmas lights with their car lights off, being guided only by the luminaries along the road. There were several hills around our town, and we would drive to the top of one of them to look down at the lights. What a beautiful sight it was! We could ascertain where various neighborhoods were even though they were several miles away. The light of those candles placed in sand inside the little white paper bags put off enough light to be seen from far away.

God wants us to be His light into the world as we carry the message of love to those we come in contact with, either directly or indirectly. I am reminded of the hymn that I learned as a child and still enjoy singing, "This Little Light of Mine." We are God's light in the world as we show the world love for everyone, and always let *our* light shine at all times!

"This little light of mine, I'm going to let it shine, let it shine, let it shine."

PRAYER: Lord, let us be Your light in the world as it prevents us from living in the darkness of the underworld. AMEN.

FOR THE BEAUTY
OF THE EARTH

GENESIS 1: 31 (NKJV) *Then God saw everything that He had made, and indeed it was very good. So the evening and the morning were the sixth day.*

As I look around at God's creations, I can't help thinking of a hymn I learned as a child and still sing, "For the Beauty of the Earth." The words include all we experience in this colorful world God created for humankind to enjoy — both that which we see alone and that which we experience with each other.

I look out my windows at magnificent trees towering high into the sky and the plants and flowers which bloom every season of the year. All of this causes me to praise our Creator. I watch birds of all colors and sizes flying around, climbing up and down the trunks of the trees, and searching on the ground for insects to eat. Then they sing to us and to each other. At night, we hear the crickets and katydids singing to us as well. All this makes me grateful for my vision and hearing.

I enjoy the flowers that bloom year 'round as the seasons change. In the advent of spring, various daffodils, tulips, crocus and many other spring flowers appear. As the spring turns to summer, other flowers appear in our yards and flowering trees put forth their beauty. As fall comes, the trees begin their presentations of various colors as they start their season of dormancy and ultimately lose their leaves. During the winter, I enjoy looking at the bare tree branches and their formations as they open to a view of the mountains in the distance. I know that in just a short while, the trees will again bring forth new leaves and blossoms to enjoy and thus the cycle begins again.

The sky is interesting with the various formations of clouds crossing its background of blue. The sunrise and sunset produce marvelous colors as the sun comes up and then once again sets allowing us to see the moon and stars. After a rainstorm, we can frequently see the rainbow that God promised those on Noah's Ark. I enjoy looking for a rainbow after a storm, and sometimes I find a double and even a triple one. The rainbow is a promise of God's greatness and protection.

God's creativity is unmatched by anything that humans can create. Creation is ongoing and not to be taken lightly by any of us but is to be enjoyed continually as we give thanks to the Creator.

PRAYER: God, we give thanks every day for the beauty of Your creation. You are ever at work fashioning beauty for us to enjoy. Sometimes out of the chaos of storms we find beauty if we just look around. Guide us to take time to look at our surroundings and enjoy the beauty and give thanks for it. AMEN.

GOD'S FACE

EXODUS 16:10 (NIV) *While Aaron was speaking to the whole Israelite community, they looked toward the desert, and there was the glory of the LORD appearing in the cloud.*

One afternoon after my mom's death, my husband and I were driving down a country road back to our home. As I looked up at the sky, I saw that the clouds had formed what looked like God's face, or what we might envision that to be. I pointed it out to my husband, and he had noticed it as well. We pulled off the road and reveled at the formation. Knowing that we will never see God in this life, it still looked like God's face in the clouds. It was so awesome! At that moment, I knew that my mom was with God in His Heavenly home. As we sat there, the clouds slowly dissipated, the formation changed and the face was no longer visible. This was before we had cell phones with cameras and we had no means of taking a picture. I wonder if we had had a camera whether the photo would have come out. For those few minutes we both were filled with such joy! I believe that God sent that cloud formation as a sign of His abiding love and as a sign that He is with us at all times.

I believe God sends signs like this to us many times, but frequently we are too busy to notice them. We need to make time in our busy schedules to notice what God is trying to tell us through sights we experience and through that "still, small voice" of the Holy Spirit that abides in each of us.

PRAYER: Help us, Lord, to take time to enjoy the beauties You have in store for us every day and give thanks for these gifts. AMEN.

GOD'S PAINTBRUSH

PSALM 19:1 (NKJV) *The heavens declare the glory of God; And the firmament shows His handiwork.*

In 2020, we faced a world-wide pandemic like nothing before. We were forced to stay in our homes, cancel trips or vacations, were unable to attend worship services, or have a casual meal with our neighbors and friends. Through it all, I have been able to admire and marvel at the beauty that surrounds us produced by God's paintbrush.

As we grumble about the things we can't do, there is still plenty for us to do. At the first of the year, I woke up to some of the most beautiful snowfalls, leaving the trees and ground, along with rooftops, covered in a canopy of white. Fortunately, it didn't last long, and I was back to my regular activities, forgetting the picture God painted for me. Then came the spring when the daffodils and other flowers were magnificent. The flowering fruit trees were profuse with blooms! They were more beautiful than I can remember. Maybe I had noticed things more while we were in a state of lock down due to the pandemic and I had taken time to look around at what God was showing me.

In summer we got rain when we needed it most, allowing our yards and gardens to stay green without us having to water them. Fall presented itself with some of the most beautiful colors I've ever seen. Some years it is so hot and dry that we only get dull brown leaves which begin to fall in the summer. This year, the leaves have stayed on the trees and turned all shades imaginable, from the yellows of the hickory trees to the brilliant reds of the maples and Bradford pears. As the sun shines on them, they glow with the paint color God has chosen for them. I have also noticed glorious sunrises and sunsets — all created by God.

What have I learned this year? I have learned that no matter what is going on, I need to take time to look at what God is showing me and what He can do to brighten my days when things around me are uncertain. He is showing me, and you, that He is ever present and has so much to give us if we just take the time to notice.

PRAYER: God, thank You for the beauty that You surround us with and help us to take time to be mindful of Your beautiful creations. AMEN.

MOUNTAINS AND VALLEYS

PSALM 121:1 (NKJV) *I will lift up my eyes to the hills– from whence comes my help? My help comes from the Lord who made heaven and earth.*

Like Jesus' disciples on the Mount of Transfiguration, we experience "mountaintop" times where we look out at the beauty all around us, take in the fresh air, and dream of staying there forever. However, these are only transitory experiences; we must return to our daily lives at some point. The climb up a mountain isn't easy and the descent won't be either. Short, steep and narrow paths open to areas that are much easier. As we start the descent, we realize that the paths we just covered are awaiting us ahead.

When the mountains are covered with snow, we see skiers fearlessly descending by jumping off one point to another. I think of the courage they have. They have studied the terrain and know where they can land safely. I wonder how they have the courage to do so, or is it courage they can only get from God? I would love to hear whether they have relied on God to be with them or whether they ski the terrain on their own.

As we descend, we continue to look at the beauty both of the mountains and the valleys below. I don't want to miss experiencing anything. A skier, on the other hand, is interested only in safely coming down the mountain as fast as possible rather than enjoying the beauty all around.

As we get closer and closer to the valley below, we may see vast meadows with flowers and flowering trees. From this vantage point, we do not see the rocks and roots that may crop up under our feet. We must keep our eyes on where we are going and rely on God directing our paths just as He did as we descended the mountain. At the same time, we can enjoy beauty surrounding us.

As our journey continues, we come upon a stream of cool refreshing water. A drink from this clear, flowing stream is refreshing after the climbing and the trek through the meadows. As we follow the stream, it seems to be widening and then becomes brisk. We see it flowing rapidly over rocks and at times see whitecaps on the water. We realize that we need to cross the stream to a safer and less treacherous part of our journey. We must rely on God showing us the way. He takes our hand and gently shows us where to put our feet as we cross this stream.

Along the way, we hear the birds singing, we see fish swimming in the stream, and frogs and turtles playing in the water, smell the sweet scents of the flowers and trees, and see animals romping in the meadow. We have experienced so much of God's creation that we need to take time to lift praise to our Creator and give thanks for all we've seen, and for guiding our footsteps. What a privilege it is to be part of God's creation!

Along life's journey, we will experience mountaintop wonders and enjoy the beauty of the valleys and streams of our lives. The journey isn't always easy, but we can be assured that God is with us to guide and direct our ways and protect us from dangers that lie ahead. We will come to forks in the road and at times may take the wrong path, but He will be there to lead us back on the right path and to protect us if we only rely on Him!

PRAYER: Thank You, God, for Your magnificent creations! May we take time to enjoy all the beauty that surrounds us whether we are on the mountaintop looking down or looking from the valley back at the mountain. We may be wandering among the beautiful meadows and streams. Wherever we are, You created it all! Thanks be to God. AMEN

SEASONAL CHANGES

ECCLESIASTES 3:1 (NLT) *To everything there is a season. A time for every purpose under heaven.*

As the heat of summer eases into a cooler fall season, we notice the trees and plants going dormant for the winter. This process brings another pleasing time of the year when we see fall colors all around us. The birds prepare to fly south for the winter; squirrels, chipmunks, and other critters store up nuts and other foods for the winter; the deer's coats begin to darken so they may more easily hide in the woods during the winter. Leaves turn various colors and fall along with acorns from the oak trees.

It won't be long until winter arrives. It seems to be a resting time. When the weather is too cold to do many of our outside activities, we rest as the plants and animals do. Winter is also a time for us to reflect.

After the cold of the winter, we begin to feel the warmer spring air and experience the new growth that it brings. We see new green leaves and a resurgence of plants and flowers and grasses. This is one of my favorite seasons of the year as I see all the new growth and new beginnings.

Next comes the summer with its full growth of plants, trees, flowers, grasses, and fruits we enjoy. Summer activities are in full swing: golf, tennis, water activities, and vacations. Schools are out, and children are home again.

Before long, the cycle will begin again. God has provided for these seasonal changes. We see similar changes in ourselves as we grow older and, we hope, wiser with each passing year. Many of us are in the fall of our lives, moving toward winter when we will have time to rest from our labors and delve deeper into God's Word.

PRAYER: Thank You, God, for providing us with the seasonal changes as we are able to enjoy times of growth and rest not only through Your creation, but in our lives as well. Keep us ever mindful that there is a season for all things and to enjoy every season whether it is all around us or within our own bodies. AMEN.

WALKING IN THE WOODS

PSALMS 104:24 (NIV) *How many are your works, LORD! In wisdom you made them all; the earth is full of your creatures.*

Where I live, we have miles of hiking trails, most of which are in the woods. Every fall there is a hiking marathon when we have a month to hike 26.2 miles on the trails. Each year the trails for the marathon are different, so obviously there are literally miles of trails. The trails have been built and continue to be built and maintained by volunteers. They vary in length from a couple of miles to several miles, and some connect with others to offer longer hikes. Some are steep and difficult; some meander gently through the woods. Each trail is marked so hikers won't get lost and will come out where they expect to. These markers also let emergency crews know where hikers are in case someone is injured or needs medical care.

As I walk these trails (even on the difficult ones) feeling the breeze and communing with nature, I relax. Tall pines and oaks provide a canopy to the ground and all the creatures that live there. As I walk, I may see deer which are plentiful in our community, chipmunks, squirrels, and various small critters. Fortunately, I have never come upon snakes, which are by far my least favorite creature.

Wild flowers grow throughout the year, along with ferns of various varieties, rhododendrons, mosses, and many other ground covers whose names I do not know. Beautiful rock formations provide opportunities to climb or rest. On some of the trails, creeks alongside bubble and provide a pleasant background soundtrack.

Some people go for a hike in the woods and rush to finish, but I like to stroll and enjoy the beauty that God created for us to enjoy. It is a pleasure to be out in the woods, even though I have to spray for insects that may bite, and watch for poison ivy. Listening to the birds and other critters is also enjoyable.

Other places in this country and around the world provide similar enjoyment, unlike big cities with no woods or natural settings to escape to. I am glad I live where I can enjoy nature as God intended us to do. How marvelous are His creations!

PRAYER: Wherever we are, there is natural beauty that You created for us to enjoy. Lord, help us to take time from our busy schedules to enjoy that beauty as we open our eyes and ears to it and to give thanks for Your creations. AMEN.

WONDERS OF THE WORLD

GENESIS 1:1 (NIV) *In the beginning God created the heavens and the earth.*

GENESIS 1:31 (NIV) *God saw all that he had made, and it was very good.*

Recently, my husband and I spent part of our vacation in Chattanooga, Tennessee. I grew up not far from Chattanooga and visited some of the sights there as a young child. I also grew up when you saw signs on roof tops of barns saying, "See Rock City". It had been over sixty years since I had been a tourist in Chattanooga so we made a list of all the sights to visit, some old and some new. We visited Rock City, Ruby Falls, traveled up the mountainside on the incline railroad, drove around on Signal Mountain overlooking the city and valley below, and visited the Chattanooga Choo-Choo. There were other points of interest such as the Chattanooga Aquarium, the Hunter Art Museum, the original Crystal Hamburger store, the Moon Pie General Store, and the train museum. We found Chattanooga full of great places to visit, but at the top of the list were Rock City and Ruby Falls.

I had visited Rock City as a child, but didn't remember much, other than you could see seven different states on a clear day from the look-out point. The rock formations were amazing as we wandered around the grounds. I had never been to Ruby Falls, which is the nation's tallest and deepest underground waterfall open to the public. We rode an elevator down to the lower level of the massive cave. When we reached the falls, I was aghast at the beauty deep down in this cave. How God had created it is unknown to us and it was discovered less than a hundred years ago, but is now visited by half a million people a year. It is amazing to see these underground creations that God has made for our enjoyment, and how He continues to reveal them to us as time goes on.

This trip gave me a greater appreciation of God's wonders both above and below the ground.

PRAYER: God, we give thanks for all the beauties of creation You have given to us. Some are right before our eyes while others are deep in the earth, only discovered by an inquisitive mind given someone by our great Creator. AMEN.

LIVE LIKE YOU WERE DYING

FIRM FOUNDATION

MATTHEW 7: 24-27 (NIV) *Therefore everyone who hears these words of mine and puts them into practice is like a wise man who built his house on the rock. The rain came down, the streams rose, and the winds blew and beat against that house; yet it did not fall, because it had its foundation on the rock. But everyone who hears these words of mine and does not put them into practice is like a foolish man who built his house on sand. The rain came down, the streams rose, and the winds blew and beat against that house, and it fell with a great crash.*

When we decided to build our current home, the land on which we would build was primarily rock. We had to bring in fill-dirt in order to shore up the footings for the house. The foundation built on this rock is truly a firm foundation that won't wash away when storms come. We also are on the highest point on our street which gives us protection from flooding.

Thinking of our house reminds me of the nursery rhyme about the three little pigs building their houses. One built its house out of straw; and when the wolf came and huffed and puffed, he blew the house down. The next one built its out of sticks; and when the wolf came and huffed and puffed, he blew this house down as well. The third pig built its house out of brick; and when the wolf tried to blow it down, it stood firm.

These stories can remind us to build our earthly homes on a firm foundation so that no "wolf" can blow it down, but they also remind us of how we build our spiritual homes. We want to ultimately dwell in an eternal home with our Lord and Savior. If we focus on that, when our life on earth comes to a close, we will be assured of an eternal home. We prepare for our eternal home by studying the Bible and believing in the birth, life, death and resurrection of Jesus Christ. Our earthly home lasts for only a short period of time, and then we return to our Maker for eternity. I want my earthly home and my eternal one to be built on a firm foundation. Don't you?

PRAYER: Help us to build both our earthly home and our eternal home on a firm foundation so that when we die, we are assured of spending eternity with You. AMEN.

LEAVING

JOHN 14:3 (NIV) And *if I go and prepare a place for you, I will come back and take you to be with me that you also may be where I am.*

Recently, a dear friend lost the love of her life and told me she didn't know how she would go on without his sweet smile, infectious humor and the enduring love they had for each other. This is how most of us feel about our loved ones when they pass on to live in eternity with our Lord and Savior in the place He has prepared for us. It is never easy to say, "Good-bye" to them, even though we know they are going to a better place that God has been preparing for them throughout their lives. We all know that we are not immortal and that someday we will no longer walk around on this earth. Still, we put that concept into the back of our minds so that we do not have to deal with it now!

I imagine the disciples felt the same way some two-thousand years ago when they experienced Jesus being crucified. He had been preparing them for this very moment for quite some time, but just like us, they just didn't get it. I can imagine the loss they felt at that time. They had given up their careers to follow this man and travel throughout the area from Galilee to Jerusalem. They had listened to Jesus teach both themselves as well as the multitudes that followed Him. When the time came for Jesus to return to the Father, what did they do? They ran and hid so the same result would not happen to them. They grieved for their leader and worried about their own lives all the while remembering the close fellowship they had with Jesus previously.

Grief is part of our daily living. We not only grieve the loss of loved ones, we grieve over the loss of a job, physical health, sight, diagnosis of cancer or any other debilitating disease that causes us to make life changes and decisions. How we deal with grief is the key to how we continue to live our lives without a loved one or with the life changes that happen to us. Once we were young and had all the energy imaginable, and expectations for our lives were endless. As we grow older the energy lessens and we have done away with many expectations we had in our younger years. Life has changed and we are moving on to our eternal home. Jesus promised that the Father would leave an advocate for us — the Holy Spirit. He is with us every day in everything we do! Praise the Lord!

PRAYER: Lord, we know that grief is not easy to deal with. That is why You left us the Holy Spirit to be with us throughout our lives. Help us to recognize Your presence through the Holy Spirit as we go through our lives and deal with the different kinds of grief and loss that we are confronted with, knowing that You have prepared a place with You for every one of us who believes. AMEN.

PASS IT ON

2 TIMOTHY 2:2 (NKJV) *And the things that you have heard from me among many witnesses, commit these to faithful men who will be able to teach others also.*

When visiting the Holy Land years ago, one thing I noticed was the drastic contrast between the Sea of Galilee and the Dead Sea which are connected by the Jordan River. Both seas are below sea level, but one is alive and the other dead. What is the difference?

We traveled from the Sea of Galilee to the Dead Sea, following the Jordan River as it meanders from north of the Sea of Galilee into the Sea of Galilee, and on south into the Dead Sea where it ends. The Sea of Galilee and Jordan River are brimming with fish and other fresh water life, whereas the Dead Sea, due to the salt content, does not support any life. As you look at the Sea of Galilee, it is fed by fresh water coming into it from the Jordan and then the water flows out, keeping the Sea constantly being refreshed. As you get to the Dead Sea, water only flows into it but not out and the water mixes with the salt from the surrounding water basin and "dies", so to speak.

In comparison to our lives, we receive God's love and need to share it with those around us. If we only take in God's love, mercy and grace and do not share it with others, we too become stagnant and "die" as the Dead Sea does. God created us to be His children and to show our love to others as He pours it out on us. We need to be continually "fed" with God's living water in order to share it with others.

I am reminded of the hymn, "Pass it On." As I receive God's love, I want to pass it on so that others may experience what I have received. I don't want to become like the Dead Sea.

PRAYER: Lord, as we receive Your love, mercy and grace, teach us to pass it on to those we encounter in our life's journey so that others may know You and all You have in store for them if they will accept it. AMEN.

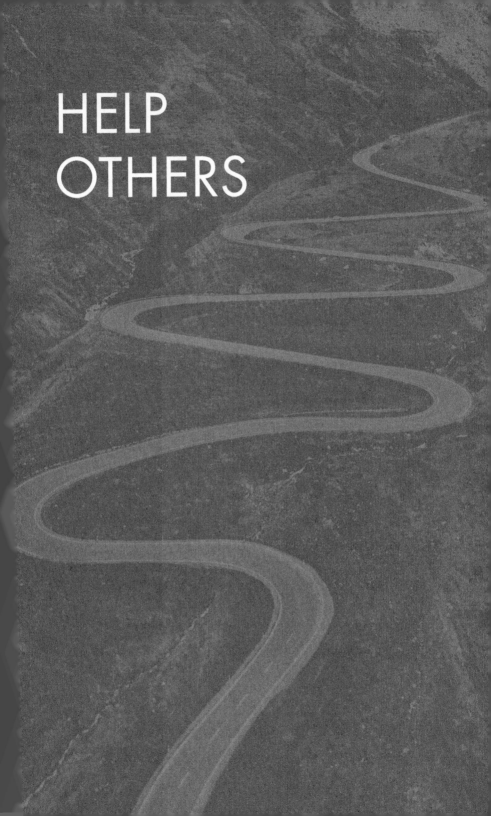

A BETTER LIFE

MATTHEW 25:23 (NLT) *His master replied, "Well done, good and faithful servant! You have been faithful in handling this small amount, so now I will give you many more responsibilities. Let's celebrate together!"*

As I grow older and stronger in my faith, I begin to think of how I will be remembered when I die. Will I have had a positive effect upon another's life? Will God be able to say, "Well done, good and faithful servant. Come live with Me for eternity."?

There are those who have made a lasting impact on this world as we know it today. We can recall Benjamin Franklin discovering electricity and how that discovery has had an impact on the whole world. We enter into a dark room and flip a switch and have light. Louis Pasteur discovered penicillin which has saved millions of lives since its discovery. Jonas Salk discovered the polio vaccine saving people's lives around the world by eradicating polio. These giants left a legacy that has improved so many lives. We can't all be a Franklin, Pasteur, or Salk, but we can live lives that impact others and make this world a better place to live.

I hope that when I die, I will have lived a life that helped others by having shown God's love to them. Just think, if we all lived a life helping others and loving others, what a different world this would be! If we could eradicate hate and violence by showing a little more love to those who would do evil, their lives and the lives of those around them might be different.

PRAYER: Lord, show me how I can help those around me and make their lives better by just living the life You want each of us to live — a life of caring for others and showing them the love You taught us to have for them. AMEN.

A GOOD SHEPHERD

PSALM 91:11-12 (NIV) *For He will command His angels concerning you to guard you in all your ways. On their hands they will bear you up, lest you strike your foot against a stone.*

Years ago, my husband and I had an experience I will always remember. We were returning home from a walk when a car pulled up beside us. The driver lowered his window and asked us if we knew the young child in the passenger's seat. Looking into the car, we recognized our neighbor's three-year-old son. We called him by name and he just grinned. We also recognized the driver as a Tennessee Titan. He told us he had been leaving our neighborhood and noticed this child wandering by himself along the parkway. He picked him up and began trying to locate the parents and return this child to them. We were almost at our home and the child lived directly across the street from us. We walked there with the car following us. As we arrived at the house, the neighbors pulled up in their driveway. They were shocked when they heard the story since their older daughter was supposed to be babysitting her brother. He had slipped out of the house and had wandered away by himself.

As I think back, it was God's protective hand that put this football player in the right place at the right time and also that we knew the child and were able to guide him back to his parents. Thank God for this good shepherd! We hear frequently in the news about children being abducted while playing in their own front yard. Many times, their stories end up differently. This does not mean to say that God wasn't with them; it's just that there are evil persons in this world. We all must keep our eyes open and be willing to work as God's messengers to care for children as well as adults that cross our paths.

PRAYER: Father, be with us when we see a need in others and show us how to be a good shepherd by protecting Your flock from harm that others may cause. AMEN.

BREAD OF LIFE

MATTHEW 25:34-40 (NKJV)... *for I was hungry and you gave Me food; I was thirsty and you gave Me drink; I was a stranger and you took Me in; I was naked and you clothed Me; I was sick and you visited Me; I was in prison and you came to Me.... inasmuch as you did it to one of the least of these My brethren, you did it to Me.'*

Our community opened a shelter many years ago called the Bread of Life where homeless people can come for a place to sleep out of the cold or heat and receive hot meals. The men and women along with their children may stay there until they can move out into a home of their own. These individuals or families are not only fed hot meals; they are also fed the Word of God in worship services held every evening. They are also assisted in obtaining jobs so they can save money to get their own home. When they are able to move into their own place, the Bread of Life helps provide them with furniture and other household items necessary for daily living.

This shelter is self-sustaining through donations and gifts from individuals and churches, relying on no government subsidy. Many church groups provide meals for the residents on a rotating basis. When the group provides the meals, they also interact with the residents throughout the meal. The ministry operates a thrift store which employs some of the residents and is also the source of many items they need for their own daily living.

Our former church provided an evening meal, a place to sleep at night during cold weather, a breakfast and a sack lunch for those without a home. As we sat and talked with these people, it was amazing to learn that many of them had college educations and had held good jobs, but circumstances such as job loss, health conditions, or drug addiction had caused them to become homeless. We don't know what has gone on in the lives of the people, but we can help them during this time. As the scripture tells us, when we do for those in need, we are doing it for the Lord.

PRAYER: Our Father, You have provided so much for Your children, but there are still those who need additional help. Help those of us for whom much has been given to share our bounty with those less fortunate. Keep us from looking down on those less fortunate and love them as You have loved us. AMEN.

FUTURE PLANS

JEREMIAH 29:11 (NIV) *"For I know the plans I have for you," declares the LORD, "plans to prosper you and not to harm you, plans to give you hope and a future."*

How many times do you experience people crossing your path when you least expect it? As I write this devotion, I am sitting in the doctor's office waiting for my husband to have tests done. Sitting beside me is a woman who is writing on her computer, too. We spoke and shared what each is writing. She is working on a book to help children develop life skills that will be with them and enable them to have self-confidence in order to be successful in life. She has worked with at-risk children and watched them grow as they learned to not let the experiences of their past and present dictate their future. As we talked, we shared experiences of our respective pasts and how our parents had raised us to become the persons we are today.

As guardian *ad litem* for dependent and neglected children in the Juvenile Court system, I saw many children who had no expectations beyond what their parents were doing. I shared how I had worked with many of these children who have come from abusive situations in their families. Many of them end up in the same situations as their families, or even worse. With the right guidance from teachers, counselors, and others who come into their lives, they can become able to see a future beyond what they otherwise would envision. I have known children in the foster-care system whose foster parents or adoptive parents empowered them so that they looked forward to going to college and becoming teachers, lawyers, nurses, or entering many other occupations. Working with those who were close to finishing high school, we were able to connect them with scholarship money to enable them to go to college. Someone showing these vulnerable youth that they have worth and a future will often open their eyes to a new world.

We are all worthwhile, and God has plans for each of us, to prosper us and to give us hope for the future.

PRAYER: Help us to find those who need help with believing in themselves and learning that they are Your precious creations, Lord. We are never too old to make a positive impression on another's life and give them the self-esteem to be who You created them to be. AMEN.

GOD'S CHILDREN

PROVERBS 22:6 (NIV) *Start children off on the way they should go, and even when they are old they will not turn from it.*

Our children are not our possessions but God's. He has given us the responsibility to raise these children in a manner pleasing to Him. He entrusts us with these precious beings when they are unable to care for themselves, and we as parents have to nurture them, feed and clothe them, and provide for their every need. As children grow older, they learn to crawl and walk and then to feed themselves. Our responsibility as parents extends to protecting them from things that may harm them. Along the way, we must exercise proper discipline in training them and teaching them right from wrong.

In those early years, it seems like not sleeping through the night will never end, and in the blink of an eye, that child is going to pre-school and then first grade. We look back and can't imagine where time has gone. As they grow older, they are faced with many decisions in life and sometimes we have to exercise "tough love" in dealing with situations they get themselves into. Before long they are driving and planning for high school graduation, as well as for college or a career on their own. At this time, our immediate responsibility of raising these precious children is ending, and they are assuming the role of an adult.

We have to let them go to learn from their own mistakes rather than trying to protect them from everything that happens to them. During the tumultuous teen years, there is an inward struggle going on as they struggle with still being a child and growing into adulthood at the same time. They are young adults and not children any more. A friend once told me that the teen years are part of that process and as they mature into their early twenties, they become more a friend to us. They are still our children, but then they have to take responsibility for their actions. We are always there to love and comfort them in difficult times, but we must let them grow on their own. We hope that they will remember all they learned while under our roof and make right choices.

PRAYER: Lord, You loaned these children to us to raise in a manner pleasing to You. As they mature and grow older, enable them to remember the teachings of their childhood, so that they make the right choices as adults. AMEN.

GRACENOTES

ISAIAH 41:10 (NKJV) *"Fear not, for I am with you; Be not dismayed, for I am your God. I will strengthen you, yes, I will help you, I will uphold you with My righteous right hand."*

When I was going through treatments for cancer, my former church started sending me notes from their card ministry. I received a card of encouragement twice a month from various members. Some of the writers I had known and others not. These cards meant much to me during that period of time. I also received many cards from friends both in our community and from far away, even from friends out of the country. I treasured every one of the cards and have them in a notebook where I can go through and re-read them when I need encouragement.

When I completed my treatment and the chemo had cleared from my brain, I felt like our church needed this ministry as well. There are many persons who for years have sent cards to those going through loss of a loved one, or during illnesses and recovery. I approached our pastors with the idea of a card ministry for our church. I also spoke with several friends about whether they would be interested writing for this ministry. I received positive feedback from everyone.

My first task was to introduce it to the congregation and enlist writers. The Sunday I presented the idea to our congregation I was hoping to get 5-10 writers. By the time I was ready to launch the ministry, I had over twenty-five writers! We send cards to the homebound, those who are ill and those who are grieving. Today, we send out over a hundred cards a month by approximately thirty writers. Each year we lose a few writers, but there are those who want to be added to take their place.

To hear from the recipients who send notes back to the church or people stopping me and telling me how much the cards meant to them has shown how much this ministry means to our congregation. From the cards I received has come a ministry that is giving to many others. God works in miraculous ways, upholding us with His righteous right hand!

PRAYER: Father, bless those who send notes of encouragement to those in need and those who receive these notes. AMEN.

HE IS ALWAYS WITH US

DEUTERONOMY 31:6 (NJKV) *Be strong and of good courage, do not fear nor be afraid of them; for the LORD your God, He is the One who goes with you. He will not leave you nor forsake you.*

The world is dealing with a pandemic like never seen before. COVID-19 has spread across the world with deaths in the tens of thousands and positive cases in hundreds of thousands. People over the world are under quarantine: businesses have had to alter their work practices, schools have had to close, causing students to have to go to virtual learning to complete their semester's work, places of worship have cancelled services, financial markets are taking a major hit, sporting and entertainment events have been cancelled. Our lives have been forever altered.

Some may ask, "Where is God in all this chaos?" He is right here among us with the medical personnel treating patients, with the doctors and scientists working on vaccines, with our country's leaders making decisions to protect those who have not contracted the virus; with the families who have lost loved ones; with our church leaders working to keep their congregations supported through new means of worship; through phone calls to church members to check on their needs. People are reaching out to neighbors who can't leave their homes to get to the groceries and pharmacies for much needed food and medications. Restaurants are using drive-through services. Everyone is affected by the times we are going through yet God's hand is seen everywhere we look.

We all need to preserve some of these experiences for future generations so that they know and understand why things are the way they are in their lifetimes. They need to know how to deal with another pandemic, if it occurs again.

This is also a time when we need to turn our thoughts to God and know that He is right here in the middle of everything we are experiencing and that He will never leave us nor forsake us.

PRAYER: May we continue to learn to help others as Jesus taught us during his time here on this earth when circumstances cause others to be in need of help by delivering food and keeping in contact with those who are unable to do for themselves. AMEN.

HUMMINGBIRDS

HEBREWS 13:2 (NIV) *Do not forget to show hospitality to strangers, for by so doing some people have shown hospitality to angels without knowing it.*

As I sat on our deck one afternoon, my husband noticed a hummingbird buzzing around my shoulder looking for a place to drink from, noticeably my ear! I had a hot pink shirt on and he may have thought I was a large feeder! My husband shooed the hummingbird away before he stuck his proboscis into my ear. This started me wondering — wondering how that small hummingbird finds feeders, wondering where and when they sleep, whether they have nests and how they reproduce little ones. There is so much about the habitat and life of the hummingbird that I don't know. The one thing I do know is that God created the hummingbird as He did me and He will provide for it just as He does for all His living creatures.

After being mistaken for a feeder, we purchased a hummingbird one and put it outside our breakfast room window where we can watch the birds that have taken up residence around it. We watch them come and go, stopping for a drink of the sweet hummingbird nectar then chasing each other. There does seem to be a leader who sometimes sits as sentinel in the closest tree. When another bird comes to the feeder, the lookout immediately flies down and off they go! It's as if this is **his** feeder and nobody else can drink there.

Have you ever experienced someone else claiming that a chair, seat, or even a church pew was theirs? There are stories about visitors going to a new church and being ask to move because "This is *my* seat." Do you think that visitor will ever come back to that church? This also happens at other places as well. We need to be welcoming and gracious when new people come into our presence. Do you think God is happy when we claim our place and do not welcome strangers? These are some things to think about.

PRAYER: Father, make us ever mindful of strangers who may come into our presence and make them welcome, for in doing so, we don't know who we may be entertaining. AMEN.

JUST DO IT

1 CHRONICLES 28:20 (NKJV) *And David said to his son Solomon, "Be strong and of good courage, and do it; do not fear nor be dismayed, for the LORD God—my God—will be with you. He will not leave you nor forsake you, until you have finished all the work for the service of the house of the LORD.*

How many times did you hear your parents tell you when you were growing up to "Just do it" when you were trying to justify not doing something? It may have been something as simple as making your bed, carrying out the trash, setting the table, washing the dishes, or other tasks. From childhood, we have practiced the act of trying to get out of doing something we don't want to do. As parents, we also find that our children are no different than we were when we were children. Even today, we are still practicing that act of trying to avoid doing something that we don't want to do. Instead of making excuses, we need to "Just do it!" A lot of times just doing something takes less time than spending time trying to justify not doing it.

So it is with God and our relationship with Him. God sometimes taps us on the shoulder and wants us to do something as simple as calling a neighbor or friend, visiting someone ill, or just sending a card. You may be called to do something far greater than these simple things. Maybe, instead of making excuses as to why we aren't doing what God is asking us to do, we should . . . "Just do it!"

PRAYER: God, we know that You will never ask us to do things that we are not equip to do and that You will be there by our side to help us along the way whatever the task may be. We need to listen to You and just do whatever it is You are calling us to do. AMEN.

KEEP YOUR EYE
ON THE BALL

PSALM 16:11 (NIV) *You make known to me the path of life; you will fill me with joy in your presence, with eternal pleasures at your right hand.*

I was a tennis player from my teen years until I injured my ankle later in life. One thing that I learned early in my tennis playing was to keep your eye on the ball. If you don't, you give up the chance of winning the match. The ball can go flying past you and the chance you have to return it is quickly gone, or it may hit and injure you.

Life is similar to tennis in that when we don't keep our eye on the ball, it can pass you by and you miss out on the joys life has to offer.

The choices you have in tennis are: (1) you can stand at the net and get hit; (2) you can let the ball go past you and depend on your partner to hit it; or (3) you can get involved and race for the ball, putting it in a place where your opponents can't get to it. All the time you need to be keeping your eye on the ball and on your opponents so that when the opportunity arises you can score your point and win the game.

In life, there are those who just stand still and end up harming themselves because they are afraid to protect themselves when harm comes their way; there are those who depend on someone else to do the job; or there are those who get involved in whatever may present itself and help others rather than just standing still.

It is my belief that God wants all of us to choose the third option and get involved where He leads us. By doing this, we can accomplish many great things in life. Life is all about living it to its fullest. That is why God put us on the earth to enjoy the great gifts He has given us and to help others enjoy them as well.

PRAYER: Lord, help us to remember to keep our eye on the ball and live life to its fullest helping others do likewise. AMEN.

LET YOUR LOVE RIPPLE ACROSS YOUR LIFE

MATTHEW 7:12 (NIV) *So in everything, do to others what you would have them do to you, for this sums up the Law and the Prophets.*

We should always be aware of how we treat others and how our actions affect those around us. Our love ripples out over other lives like a small rock thrown out on a still body of water. Those ripples go on and on, and so should our love.

When I first started practicing law, I had a couple of clients who referred others to me. They in turn referred still others. And so, my practice grew, primarily by word of mouth. I can trace much of it back to those first clients. I always treated each client as I had been treated previously by my attorney. He was informative, patient, and understanding even when I was having a bad day. My practice was primarily family law dealing with divorce, custody, and child support. Having been through a divorce myself, I knew how these clients felt and what they were going through. When I finished law school in my late 40's, the last area of law I wanted to deal with was family law. However, I feel God led me into this field since I could relate to these clients. I recognized myself so many times in the men and women who sat across from me in my office. My prior experiences enabled me to effectively assist them through the legal process. Being understanding with my clients is similar to that rock sending ripples across the still body of water. That is how God's love is. We treat others the way we would like to be treated, and they in turn, hopefully, will do likewise with those they meet, sending out more ripples of God's love.

PRAYER: Lord, let us always be mindful of others in their needs and feelings, always showing the love and understanding You have taught us to have for them. May that love send ripples across our lives into the lives of those with whom we come in contact, thus spreading Your love throughout the world. AMEN.

MENDING FENCES

EPHESIANS 4:32 (NKJV) *And be kind to one another, tenderhearted, forgiving one another, even as God in Christ forgave you.*

As you drive down a highway or back road where there is pasture land, you will frequently see farmers out mending the fences. This is done to keep livestock in their pastures and not out grazing where they aren't supposed to graze. As time goes on, the fences will become damaged and need to be repaired or replaced. Sometimes the fences are to keep others out of the pasture or off the property. Recently, we were traveling on a major interstate and alongside the road a cow was grazing not far off the shoulder of the road. I called the highway patrol to report the cow being on the interstate. I was not the first to report it. It was remarkable that the cow had not been hit by a car or truck, causing damage to the animal and vehicle and some of its passengers.

Just as the farmer or landowner needs to mend fences, so we must do with those with whom we come in contact. Relationships need care so that we do not harm our family, friends and neighbors. If we fail to think before we act or speak, we can harm others without even knowing it. An old saying tells us "Engage your brain before you engage your mouth."

We need to consider every day what we will do to maintain our good relationships with those around us. And when we hurt someone, or they hurt us, pray about that relationship and ask God to show us a way to "mend the fences" with our family or friends. He wants all of us to love one another just as Christ taught us. If we fail to mend our fences (as some farmer apparently had done when the cow got out), we too may injure others or be injured either physically or emotionally ourselves.

PRAYER: Lord, help us to recognize when we have hurt someone else and enable us to go to them and mend that relationship. Help us to remember that relationships with family and friends are some of the most important aspects of our lives, and unresolved hurts can cause long-term pain to both ourselves and others. AMEN.

PERFECT TIMING

ECCLESIASTES 3:1(NKJV) *To everything there is a season, A time for every purpose under heaven.*

Have you ever gotten the time of an appointment wrong and arrived at your destination early, only to discover that God may have had a hand in it? This happened to me recently. I thought that my appointment for a haircut was 10:00, when in fact according to both my calendar and my hairdresser's calendar, it was 11:00. While I was waiting in the salon, a church member came in for her appointment with another hairdresser. She had recently lost her husband and appeared to be having a difficult time.

Our church has a program called Stephen Ministry. Stephen Ministers are lay people trained to be care givers to those suffering loss or other crises. It is a one-on-one confidential care ministry. I was a trained Stephen Minister and as she talked, I felt drawn to suggest that she might benefit from a Stephen Minister to walk with her during her time of grief. Just as I was going to suggest that she request a Stephen Minister, she said that one of our leaders was coming by the next day to discuss Stephen Ministry with her and to have someone assigned to her. My training shifted into gear as if God was leading me and I listened to her, letting her talk about how she was feeling and to discuss her husband's sudden death. I also suggested she might benefit from our Grief Share Group, which she had already looked into.

After my haircut, I again apologized to my hairdresser for coming at the wrong time. Both of our hairdressers told me that God had intended for me to be early and to be there to speak with a friend from church. It was God's perfect timing that had led me to come an hour early.

PRAYER: Lord, we never know when You will place us in a position where we can listen and share Your love with others and comfort those who are hurting. We know that if we listen to Your calling, we will be where You want us to be at the right time. AMEN.

RANDOM ACTS
OF KINDNESS

JOHN 3:16 (NIV) *For God so loved the world that he gave his one and only Son, that whoever believes in him shall not perish but have eternal life.*

Several years ago, the news told of a movement of random acts of kindness. People in fast food lines or grocery stores were paying the check of the person behind them. Some of the stories that came from that movement were heart-warming.

A few times I have been the recipient of such a random act of kindness. The most recent time was when we were in a sandwich shop. We got to the cash register to pay when the employee said, "Your meal has been paid for." We had seen someone in front of us, but by the time our food was ready, she was gone. Such an experience left me with the feeling that I needed to go out and find the person in order to thank them. But they were gone. What that person did for me inspires me to want to go out and do for another.

After that incident, we were dining in a local restaurant and our police chief was at the adjoining table. My husband called his waitress over and asked for the chief's bill which we paid. As he was leaving, he stopped at our table and asked if we had been the ones to pay for his meal and thanked us for it. For us, it was a small way of saying, "Thanks for what you do in protecting us every day."

Jesus did something much more amazing for all of us on the cross. He paid the ultimate price for our sins as He was crucified as the perfect sacrifice. What a wondrous gift God gave us through His Son Jesus Christ, who was willing to undergo an excruciating form of death (crucifixion) for us. "Thank You, God," seems an inadequate response to the greatest act of kindness ever given. We should always remember to give thanks for this matchless gift from our Heavenly Father!

PRAYER: Help us to remember to give thanks every day for the ultimate gift of Your Son, Jesus Christ, who gave His life that we would be saved and live with You in eternity. Help us to remember to spread random gifts of kindness as we live out our lives. AMEN.

SERVANTHOOD

JOHN 13:4-5 (NIV) ... *so he got up from the meal, took off his outer clothing, and wrapped a towel around his waist. After that, he poured water into a basin and began to wash his disciples' feet, drying them with the towel that was wrapped around him.*

My husband and I have been members of the Lions Clubs International for several years. Our motto is: WE SERVE. We go into the schools and test children from HeadStart through high school for vision and hearing. Helen Keller challenged the Lions to be "knights to the blind in the crusade against darkness" many years ago which is one of our greatest service areas. We also sponsor Strides Walk, which raises money to send children with Type 1 diabetes to a summer camp where they can enjoy being away from home with trained counselors to assist with their diabetes and be like any other child there. Diabetes is a leading cause of blindness. We collect for White Cane which assists with the blind and with leader dogs. We support the TN School for the Blind and the list goes on and on as we serve many agencies in the community through our fundraising campaigns. We collect grocery bags that are turned into plarn (plastic yarn) to make mats for the homeless.

Jesus taught his disciples that they should be servants to all. One of the most moving events I have participated in at our church has been during the Maundy Thursday service when we each would take turns washing the feet of others. Our pastor started by washing the feet of the first person and then they in turn washed the feet of the next person. Foot washing is not a common experience for our denomination. The first time we did this, I was unsure of whether or not to participate. After doing so I found it so humbling and felt so connected to Jesus at the last supper. Jesus, throughout his ministry, taught that we should be servants to all.

As Lions, we proudly wear our vests that state WE SERVE whenever we are serving. We are an example of what Jesus taught us to be, "servants to all."

PRAYER: Bless each person as they serve others in their communities and around the world as Jesus taught us to do. Also, bless those who are on the receiving end of our service that their lives may be improved. In Jesus' name, AMEN.

TOOLBOXES

---

1 CORINTHIANS 13: 4-7 (NKJV) *Love is patient, love is kind.... It bears all things, believes all things, hopes all things, endures all things.*

When you need to fix, repair, or build something tangible, where do you go first? You go to your toolbox. Most people have a toolbox at home with all sorts of tools in it. The simplest toolboxes will always have a hammer, screwdrivers, pliers, a ruler, some nails and screws. More complex toolboxes have many more tools in them with some people having even more than one toolbox.

We Christians also need to have a toolbox. This toolbox is not visible, but is one we should carry with us at all times. The tools in our God toolbox should be with us at all times to help repair, fix, or build things, as well. The things we repair, fix, or build are usually not tangible, but are very meaningful, such as relationships, both old and new. We carry with us many tools such as love, encouragement, prayer, God's Word, empathy, comfort, hope, peace, faith, patience, kindness, to name a few. All these tools work for the good, but they all must be wrapped in love. If we don't wrap our tools with love, we are not doing God's work in our lives. These are all designed to help those around us we know and some we don't know. We should have all of these tools ready to use for whenever the opportunity arises.

PRAYER: Lord, help us to keep our toolbox handy and ready for use when a situation calls for it. Help us to recognize those who are in need and show them the love that only You can provide. In Christ name, AMEN.

BE
THANKFUL

ANGELS IN OUR MIDST

PSALM 91:11 (NLT) *For he will order his angels to protect you wherever you go.*

Many years ago, I was moving into my law office on a Sunday afternoon. We had about three family members to assist in the move. My desk was on a trailer. We tried and tried to get it off the trailer, up a curb, and onto a dolly, to no avail. The desk was extremely heavy and very difficult to maneuver. After a while a homeless man appeared and asked if he could help. Almost by himself, he unloaded the desk, got it onto the dolly, took it into my office and unloaded it for us.

As we were going into the building, I commented on his T-shirt which had the cross and flame logo of the United Methodist Church. I asked if he was a Methodist. He told me that he attended a church in the inner-city. It just so happened that this church was a sister church of our congregation. Being in the inner-city, this church served folks from the homeless community to college professors and students - a wide range of constituents. Years ago, this had been an active neighborhood church, but due to suburban flight, it had become unable to support itself. One of the larger suburban churches had partnered with this congregation to support it financially along with the ministry in this area of town. Different groups from our church rotated attending this church and serving lunch to those who stayed after the worship service. This gentleman told me that he regularly attended this particular church, but had missed the bus that Sunday. I told him that we had just come from serving lunch at this church.

After the furniture was unloaded, my husband was going to offer him some money, but he had disappeared just as he had appeared! We looked for him and there was no sign of him anywhere. What a coincidence! Or was it? No, it was not a coincidence; we believe he was one of God's angels!

We must always be aware of God placing angels on our paths when we are in need. In fact, if we choose to be aware, there are angels all around us. All we have to do is to be open and willing to see and acknowledge them.

PRAYER: Father, thank You for sending Your angels to assist and protect us when we are in need of help. Let us always be aware of these angels when they appear. AMEN.

ATTITUDE OF GRATITUDE

MATTHEW 7:12 (NIV) *So in everything, do to others what you would have them do to you, for this sums up the Law and the Prophets.*

How often do you go through the day with an attitude of gratitude? We all need to learn to practice this more often and see how the relationships we have with others change - both how we respond to others and, in return, how they respond to us.

When we say "thank you" for even the smallest acts others do for us, we are exhibiting a positive attitude toward them. I remember how my mother taught me to say "please" and "thank you" for all the many acts others did to or for me when I was a young child. Today, many children, as well as adults, just go on their merry way without acknowledging acts of kindness. This makes the person doing the act of kindness feel that they have been ignored and not appreciated. How much energy does it take to say a simple "thank you" to another? It is not only comforting to the recipient but makes that person feel worthwhile. There are times I hear those words and don't even realize that I had done something worthwhile for another, but their acknowledgment made me feel good and I know whatever I did for another made them feel good. Isn't this what we learned as children, to "do unto others as you would have them do unto you?"

With an attitude of gratitude being utmost in our daily interactions with others, we sometimes lift those persons out of what may have been a bad day for them. Everyone needs to be appreciated. A simple act of appreciation may just empower them to appreciate others. This is how the attitude of gratitude can spread from one person to another by simply saying "thank you."

PRAYER: Father, we thank You for giving Your Son Jesus Christ to forgive our sins. What greater gift can a father give to his children. May we spend our lives being thankful for even the smallest of gifts from others and always remember to say, "thank you" for these gifts as we lift others by acknowledging them. AMEN.

DIFFICULT TIMES

ROMANS 5:3-5 (NIV) *Not only so, but we also glory in our sufferings, because we know that suffering produces perseverance; perseverance, character; and character, hope. And hope does not put us to shame, because God's love has been poured out into our hearts through the Holy Spirit, who has been given to us.*

Where do you go when difficult times hit? Many people turn to the only one who can care for us and provide for us— our Lord and Savior. Some may choose to run away from God, blaming God for all that has happened to them. What do you think about how they turn out? Many become miserable, cranky old people without many friends. Their attitude turns people away from them and they become loners.

When hard times have happened to me, I have adopted the attitude of why *not* me? What makes me better than anyone else? What have I done to deserve a problem-free life? Paul gives me encouragement through the above scripture. Without hope how would any of us get through the difficult times. Paul had many difficult times in his life, but he went on preaching the gospel, knowing that his faith and hope would help him endure the persecutions and imprisonments he faced, and finally his death.

Consider what Jesus had to endure the last few days of his life. He was accused of blasphemy, tried, and sentenced to death on a cross. He was beaten and scourged before being placed on a cross. He knew what his mission in life was, but even in the Garden of Gethsemane, Jesus pleaded with God, "Let this cup pass from me." I am reminded that He endured all these indignities for me and you! What have I done to deserve this ultimate sacrifice? I return to the first question: Where do you go when difficult times hit? As for me, I have no place to go other than to the feet of Jesus, giving thanks for all I have, regardless of how difficult the times may be.

PRAYER: Lord, keep me in Your arms when difficult times come to me. Keep me from passing blame on You or others and becoming an unpleasant person to be around. AMEN.

DOORS

REVELATION 3:20 (NKJV) *Behold, I stand at the door and knock; if anyone hears My voice and opens the door, I will come in to him and will dine with him, and he with Me.*

Doors, doors, doors, everywhere! There are doors to enter places and doors to exit. We encounter doors everywhere we go — in our homes, workplaces, dining, or other activities. The doors generally swing open for us to enter and close after we enter. Sometimes we go through a door knowing what is on the other side; sometimes we do not know what is beyond a door, but go through it anyway.

God sent His Son into the world to show us the way to salvation. Jesus stands at the door of our heart knocking and waiting for us to answer and invite Him into our lives and hearts. Do we answer the door and invite Jesus in, or do we choose to ignore Him? That is the choice we are faced with every day. The choice we make determines what our future will be.

At the time of Jesus's crucifixion, the curtain of the temple was rent from top to bottom. We might say these barriers were doors to the place the Holy of Holies resided, preventing anyone other than the High Priest, and him only, once a year to have access to the Holy Place. As Jesus was taking his last breath on the cross, the door was opened to all who would enter and worship the Lord.

When we look at the book of Revelation, we read about John being invited into the heavenly realm through the open door of heaven. There Jesus reveals to him the heavenly place with all the saints worshiping God. He also revealed to John what is to come in the future. This door to heaven stands open for everyone who chooses to worship God. Finally, Jesus reveals the New Jerusalem, which all of us who choose Jesus will see one day!

PRAYER: Father, we give thanks that through Jesus' death and resurrection, You have given to all who chose to believe in You, access to worship You individually and to approach Your throne ourselves rather than only through the High Priest. The door to heaven stands open to all of us who will believe. Thanks be to God! AMEN.

GENERATIONAL CHANGES

HEBREWS 13:8 (NIV) *Jesus Christ is the same yesterday and today and forever.*

It's amazing how things have changed since I was born! My children, and now my grandchildren, can't imagine life without cell phones, computers, cars with GPS, and all the other current day technology.

When I first learned to drive, the car was a 1947 Oldsmobile. There were no turn signals, so you used your arm to turn left or right; the changer for head lights was a button on the floor; air conditioning was opening the windows, and there were no seatbelts. Today, we have cars with all sorts of devices and even cars that can drive themselves! I wonder what tomorrow will bring to our future generations.

We had party-lines for our phones, so others on the same party-line could eavesdrop on your phone calls. We then went to our own individual phone line which was attached to the wall and had a four-digit number. You had to call the operator to make long distance calls. Today, we have ten-digit numbers and can call all over the world by punching in the numbers, and we carry our phones with us. As a child I remember Dick Tracy talking to others on his wrist phone and seeing a picture of them, which we thought was beyond belief. Today it is a reality!

I have experienced man landing on the moon. There is a space station in orbit and we have male and female astronauts traveling to and from it. Through the space program, new discoveries have been made which make life more enjoyable for us today. What will tomorrow bring? I wonder what those living a generation or two before us would think if they were to return today!

Throughout life, things change every day, but there is one constant in our lives and that is Jesus Christ. He is the same today as He was yesterday and will be tomorrow. As He watches over us, I know at times

He is saddened by our misuse of His gifts. On the other hand, He rejoices at the good things we have done with what He has provided for us!

PRAYER: Thank You, God, for all the innovations You have enabled mankind to develop. May these innovations be pleasing to You and not be used to harm others. AMEN.

GOD SO LOVED
THE WORLD

JOHN 3:16 (NKJV) *For God so loved the world that He gave His only begotten Son, that whoever believes in Him should not perish but have everlasting life.*

God created the world because He wanted to have a relationship with people. When God created Adam and Eve, He told them what was expected and what the consequences would be if they disobeyed. They chose the way of the serpent, and God inflicted the consequences. We now live in a fallen world. The Bible tells us stories of God explaining to His chosen people what would happen if they didn't follow His leading, and when they strayed, they ultimately suffered the consequence God had warned them of. God intervened with the children of Israel and led them to the Promised Land. On the way they turned from Him resulting in having to wander in the desert for 40 years. After the people arrived in the Promised Land, prophets tried to tell them what God expected of them, but over and over they rebelled and had to suffer consequences.

There were good times when the leaders, and later the kings, followed and worshiped God for a while, and then they too would turn from God, thus suffering the consequences. Finally, God decided to send His Son to the earth to teach, preach and lead His people. Jesus taught us that if we believed in Him and His Father and followed them that we would have everlasting life. What an incredible gift God gave us!

We see the actions of God's children in the Bible continuing to exist today. People never change! We all sometimes choose to turn from God rather than following His way, and we end up suffering the consequences of those choices. I've heard the old saying: "Why can't people just do right?" Well, that is part of the fallen world which goes back to Adam and Eve. However, we are assured that God still loves us and wants us to follow Him.

For God so loved the world that He gave His only begotten Son, that whoever believes in Him should not perish but have everlasting life. What a blessed assurance of God's unfailing love!

PRAYER: God, our Father, we give thanks every day for Your most precious gift— that of Your only Son who came to the earth to forgive our sins and guide and direct us to be the people You would have us to be. Thanks be to God! AMEN.

HANGING ON

MATTHEW 18:15 (NIV) *If your brother or sister sins, go and point out their fault, just between the two of you. If they listen to you, you have won them over.*

It is spring! All deciduous trees should have dropped their leaves in the fall or winter, but some of the trees in my backyard are still hanging onto their leaves. The new growth is showing on most trees, but those pesky "hanging on" leaves still haven't fallen so I can rake them away.

Do you tend to hang on to old hurts, whether they be physical, emotional, or just hurts to your feelings? Sometimes these hurts become so deeply ingrained in us that they determine how we treat others. You continually remember who did what, when, and how, thus making you unable to forgive, forget, and move on with your life. This denies happiness to so many people.

Sometimes these hurts that you hang onto affect family relationships. One family member may say something hurtful to another family member and that relationship becomes so harmed that the two don't speak to each other. Sometimes this may result in physical altercations in addition to verbal ones.

In the scripture you are advised to go to the perpetrator of the hurt and confront them, asking for forgiveness for the hurt, or perceived hurt, thus putting it to rest enabling you to move on with your life. Sometimes those persons may be deceased so you have to pray to God to enable you to forgive that person. What a freeing feeling that is! It can be compared to the new growth pushing off the "hanging on" leaves and allowing new growth to emerge.

PRAYER: Lord, we ask for You to help us forgive those who have hurt us and that we have hurt so that our relationships may be restored. AMEN.

MEMORY

MATTHEW 28:20 (NLT) .:.. *I am with you always even to the end of the age."*

In visiting with those who have lost their memory due to some form of dementia, frequently we find that when we start to pray the Lord's Prayer, say the twenty-third Psalm, or sing to them, they join in. What they learned long ago stays with them even though they cannot recognize us or know where they are or what day it is.

In a similar way, when we hear the tune of a song we had sung in church or heard on the radio, we begin to sing the words or hum along. We did not intentionally memorize those words; they have just been imprinted in our memory. I learned to play the piano at a very young age. Sometimes when we sing certain songs in church, I find my fingers playing imaginary keys on the back of the pew in front of me.

It is not a coincidence that these things happen. It is due to the Holy Spirit continuing to abide with us as long as we live, constantly reminding us of God's presence and the gifts that He has given to us.

PRAYER: Thank You, Lord, for implanting Your Word into our hearts and minds so that regardless of whether or not we are aware of our daily activities and friends, Your presence and the knowledge of You will always remain with us. AMEN.

RAIN DAYS

ECCLESIASTES 3:1-8 (NKJV) *To everything there is a season, and a time to every purpose under the heaven.*

I n my younger days, I was a stay-at-home mom. I volunteered through my church, the children's school, and in community organizations. I also played a lot of tennis, regardless of the temperature. The only thing that cancelled our games was rain (or *really* cold weather). Sometimes I needed a day just to rest, relax, and reflect, and God would at this time provide me with a rain day. When I needed that rain day, what a blessing it was! I would stay home and rest. God knew my needs better than I did, and He would say, "Rest my child. Think about Me and the things I have provided for you."

Since that time, I look forward to the unexpected "rain days" in my schedule. After I returned to the workplace, occasionally I would have nothing scheduled and I would take a "rain day." Even today when most in our community are retired, we all are involved in some type of study group, volunteer activities through the church or community, or leisure activities such as golf, tennis, fishing, book clubs, or card games. We still need a "rain day" every once in a while. We need that gift from God where we can stop and catch our breath, rest, and reflect on all the gifts God provides: the beauty of our surroundings, the season of life we are passing through, the comforts we enjoy, and most of all, our relationship with our Lord and Savior.

PRAYER: God, You have told us that there is a time for everything under heaven. Everything includes rest. If we run our bodies down, they will wear out and we are incapable of doing anything. We need to set aside time to rest and renew our bodies so that we may continue doing that which is in Your will for our lives. AMEN.

RAISING CHILDREN

PROVERBS 22:6 (NKJV) *Train up a child in the way he should go, And when he is old he will not depart from it.*

Children, especially during their teenage years, think they are so much smarter than their parents. Then as they mature into their early twenties, and sometimes into their later twenties, it's amazing at how smart their parents become! In those early years of childhood development, children are so dependent upon their parents for everything. Then as they enter their teenage years, they start pulling away and making decisions on their own, sometimes to their own detriment. I had a friend many years ago who told me how important those teen years were because they were the years where the child was letting go of the apron strings and working on being an adult, yet still wanting to hang onto the apron strings. They are in a constant state of flux between being a child and an adult at the same time. Finally, they mature enough to let go and become an adult and their relationship turns more to a parent-friend rather than parent-child. There were days when I wondered which child I was dealing with, the young child or the young adult! I know that my parents felt the same way.

As they grow older and become more independent, they realize that so many rules and guidelines their parents set for them were really important. There was a purpose in them rather than an impediment to their lives, as they thought at the time.

Have you ever sat down and written a letter to your parents to thank them for their guidance, sacrifice, and the hard work they put into raising you? For Mother's Day, the year my mother died, I wrote her a letter. I started by just saying "Thank You" which turned into a letter setting forth several things I knew that she and Daddy had done for me that I probably hadn't appreciated at the time. Later that year when she died, I found the letter tucked in her purse. You could tell that she had read it many times. I gave it to her pastor who used some of it in his eulogy. Some of her friends shared with me that she had read it to them. I was so thankful that I had taken the time before she left me to let her know how much I appreciated all she and Daddy had done for me.

PRAYER: Help us, Lord, to never forget to be thankful for all the love and sacrifices our parents made during our growing up years and beyond. AMEN.

STOP AND SMELL
THE ROSES

GENESIS 1:1 (NIV) *In the beginning God created the heavens and the earth.*

GENESIS 1:11-12 (NIV) *Then God said, "Let the land produce vegetation: seed-bearing plants and trees on the land that bear fruit with seed in it, according to their various kinds." And it was so. The land produced vegetation: plants bearing seed according to their kinds and trees bearing fruit with seed in it according to their kinds. And God saw that it was good.*

My husband and I traveled to Asheville, North Carolina, a while back, and toured the Biltmore Mansion. This was not our first time to tour the Biltmore house and gardens that surround it, but I now have more memories of this beautiful home built many years ago than I did on my first visit. We are now retired and can enjoy things differently than when we were working. We took time to soak in the beauty of our surroundings on this trip. We wandered through the gardens and the trails on the property, marveling at the flowers, plants, and trees, and even stopped to think of God's creations and how beautiful they are. Sure, there are caretakers working all around to maintain the grounds, but that would not be possible if God had not created it all. As we walked through the rose gardens, I enjoyed all the different rose plants and their flowers. I even stopped to hold several roses in my fingers and smell their beautiful aromas - I had taken time to "stop and smell the roses," as the cliché goes. We took time to wander the path to the river and enjoy the many plants and trees, paths cut into the area, rock formations and many other sights, all of which we had failed to do previously.

This experience is like our lives—we become so busy with school, careers, raising children, and trying to make a living, that we fail to take time to "stop and smell the roses" along the way. We travel down the interstate of our lives and don't see or enjoy the beauty that surrounds us every day. We fail to think where this beauty came from and to give thanks to God for all His creation. We fail to give thanks for all that He has provided for us, and instead, we become so career oriented that we miss the many things that life has to offer.

As I have grown older, I can look back and say to myself, "I wish I had taken more time to enjoy the many things that life has given me along the way." Most of all I have failed to give thanks to God for all He has given me every day. Each day is a blessing not to be taken lightly, but to be enjoyed.

PRAYER: Help us to take time to stop and smell the roses during our busy schedules. We know that You do not want us to be so busy that we fail to stop and notice the beauty of Your creation. Thank You for all Your magnificent beauty that is all around us. AMEN.

UNCERTAIN TIMES

PSALM 23:4 (NKJV) *Yea, though I walk through the valley of the shadow of death, I will fear no evil; For You are with me; Your rod and Your staff, they comfort me.*

In uncertain times the only way we can survive is through our faith and knowing that whatever the circumstances may be that God is right here with us each step of the way. At the time of this writing, this country, and the world we are living in are all dealing with a pandemic like no other that has occurred in our lifetime. There have been other viruses and flus as well as HIV/AIDS that we have lived through, but nothing of the magnitude of COVID-19.

We are faced with fear everywhere we look. Will we contract this virus? If so, will there be adequate medical equipment and hospital beds available for us? If we are high risk due to compromised immune systems, heart or lung issues, or old age, can we survive this pandemic? How long will it be before we are able to get back to our former life style? Will businesses be able to survive? Life will never be the same as we have known it after this pandemic passes. We will be faced with a new normal. We now realize that something like this virus can turn our lives upside down.

One thing I know is that God did not cause this pandemic to occur. He is, and will continue to be, with us throughout the pandemic as we try to stop or slow the spread. Times like this bring us together as neighbors and a country. We see people from all walks of life pulling together to help each other by doing simple things like going to the grocery or pharmacy for others, calling and checking on those who can't get out easily, visiting in driveways and many other ways of keeping in touch with neighbors, friends, and family. Groups all over the country are working together, yet apart, to make face masks for our medical communities, for others who need a mask to go out into public places, and for those working in the essential businesses. Large and small businesses are converting their production means to produce products that are desperately needed to care for those who have contracted the disease. It reminds me of what happened in WWII when businesses shifted to producing materials and equipment for war. Yes, this is a war, but not in the usual sense of the word.

We must remember that God will always be with us no matter what the circumstances, and He will comfort and care for us throughout whatever we face.

PRAYER: Lord, whatever the circumstances we face today, help us to remember that You are always with us. You are here in the midst of all the tragedies and joys, no matter what is going on in this world. We depend on You to wrap Your arms around us when we are suffering and comfort us in times of trials. AMEN.

VINEYARD WORKERS

MATTHEW 20:6-7 (NKJV) *And about the eleventh hour he went out and found others standing idle, and said to them, 'Why have you been standing here idle all day?' They said to him, 'Because no one hired us.' He said to them, 'You also go into the vineyard, and whatever is right you will receive.'*

I taught our Sunday school class a lesson about the vineyard workers described in the Gospel of Matthew. I have always had difficulty with this scripture about the last being first and the first being last. We see and hear of those who come to accept Christ as their Lord and Savior at the eleventh hour and who enter into Heaven just the same as those of us who accepted Christ many years before death and have lived according to His teaching for most of our lives.

As I studied the lesson about the vineyard workers, I saw them in a different way. The question asked of the workers who were last hired was, "Why have you been standing here idle all day?" Their response was, "No one had hired us." How often are there those waiting to be told the story of Jesus and to accept Him as their Lord and Savior? There are also those who choose to live their lives knowing about Jesus but choosing not to follow Him because it would change their enjoyment of their current lifestyle. Then, when the eleventh hour comes, they decide to make things right in hopes of entering into God's eternal home.

The ones who wait until the eleventh hour to confess their sins and be forgiven have missed out on much love, mercy and grace that our Heavenly Father offers. They may be accepted into their eternal home with God just as we are, but think of all they missed out on because they did not choose to follow Christ earlier. I also think of those who for some reason don't have the opportunity to accept Jesus as their Lord and Savior before they die. In the end, it doesn't matter whether we are first or last or whether we are paid the same as those who worked only the last hour. We all receive better than we deserve. None of us is worthy of all God has to give us, but His love, mercy and grace is there for everyone who seeks it and accepts it.

PRAYER: Lord, help those who have not accepted You as their Lord and Savior to come to You before the eleventh hour so that they may continue to live enjoying all the love, mercy and grace that You pour out on them when they accept You. AMEN.

CLOSER
RELATIONSHIP

ANXIETY

How often do we spin our wheels worrying about what tomorrow will bring? Will we be accepted at the right school? Will we get the new job? Will we find the right mate, and if so, will marriage be around the corner? Will we be able to have children and how many? What will they become? Will they live close by? When will we be able to retire and where will that be? These are all questions that at some point in all our lives we have asked. Some of these questions have kept us up at night worrying about them when all we need to do is to let our requests be made known to God, and then be patient for the answers and direction.

When we were young, we worried about who our teachers would be or whether we would make the sports team. We felt anxious when faced with an important test and knew we had not prepared as much as we should.

Then as we grow older some of the next questions come into play. We become anxious about having a family and job, and where we will live. Some families stay close to home with work, and others move far from their homes and family. As we progress in our work and family, we frequently learn to cope and lose the anxiety that can result. These coping mechanisms are a result of our reliance upon God guiding and directing our lives.

As we grow older, we may become anxious about retirement and whether we have put away enough money to live on. Where will we live? Will we move into a retirement community or stay where we are? Later, we have to face the probability of not being able to care for ourselves and our spouse. Do we move closer to our children? These decisions are difficult to make and cause much anxiety. The only way to cope is to call upon our Lord to lead us in the direction we need to go. This happened after my divorce when I was considering moving closer to my family. I realized that I had to turn that decision over to God. When the time was right, God provided the direction and I found peace in following His leading rather than being anxious and filled with worry.

PRAYER: Be with us, Lord, as we navigate through our life's uncertainties and give us the peace that passes all understanding as we turn our anxieties over to You. Guide and direct us during these times when all we know to do is to turn to You. AMEN.

BABY FOOD

MATTHEW 19:13-14 (NIV) *Then people brought little children to Jesus for him to place his hands on them and pray for them. But the disciples rebuked them. Jesus said, "Let the little children come to me, and do not hinder them, for the kingdom of heaven belongs to such as these."*

When a baby is conceived the mother feeds it in the womb until the time comes for the baby to enter the world to live on his own. After birth, the mother no longer feeds the baby from her own body, unless she decides to nurse the newborn. The mother's milk contains all the nutrients needed to nourish the newborn until the baby is ready for fruits, vegetables and meats. In the event that the mother chooses not to nurse the baby, formula from a bottle can provide the nutrients needed.

As the baby matures, and needs additional nutrients, the body develops so that it can handle more complex foods. Slowly, the mother or other care giver starts introducing new foods into the baby's diet. As he is able to tolerate the smooth texture of baby food, more foods are introduced. The child moves from a bottle to drinking from a cup. As teeth come in, the child is introduced to food that is still soft but chewable. Then he graduates to solid foods.

So are our lives with our Lord and Savior. When we decide to accept Christ as our Lord and Savior, we begin to feed on His Word and grow in our walk with Him. We may be a young person or an older person, but as new Christians, we are all babies in God's eyes. We must learn to be fed just as the new baby does. We would find it hard to be fed solid foods, if we had not learned to understand the basics of our spiritual walk. Just as the baby first drinks milk, then eats soft foods, and then solid foods, so we must in our spiritual walk.

We first learn that God, our Father, loves us so much that He sent His Only Son to Earth to teach us how to love and be loved. God sacrificed His Son so that we would have everlasting life. If we don't learn this first, it is hard to know and understand so much of what we read in the Bible.

As we mature in our walk with our Lord, we learn to handle the solid food. Our spiritual journey is an ongoing process of moving from baby food to solid food.

PRAYER: Father, feed us as if we were babies as we seek to learn Your ways and what You have in store for us in our lives. AMEN.

BELIEVE

JOHN 5:7-8 (NLT) *"I can't, sir," the sick man said, "for I have no one to put me into the pool when the water bubbles up. Someone else always gets there ahead of me." Jesus told him, "Stand up, pick up your mat, and walk!"*

The story of the man at the pool of Bethesda reminds me of several people I have known during my life. There have been some who have suffered traumatic injuries resulting in their not being able to walk. Through perseverance and many months, and sometimes years, of rehabilitation many people have been able to walk again. Then, there have been others whose response was, "I can't."

When Jesus asked the man if he wanted to get well, the man responded that he had no one to put him in the pool. He was depending on someone else to intercede for him. Then Jesus told him to stand up, take his mat, and walk. He did this and then ran to tell and show what Jesus had done for him.

The key to healing is believing that God can do anything and having the faith that He will. Sometimes the answer to our healing is that what we ask for is not part of God's will. There are so many stories of people who have not been healed from the illness or injury that is apparent to all around them, but are healed in other ways, ways that only God knows. God can use our disabilities or illnesses for far greater purposes than we can imagine. We just have to believe and have faith that God knows what is best for us and what is in His will.

PRAYER: When we face physical, mental or emotional challenges, Lord be with us and help us to fight to overcome those challenges by doing not just waiting for someone else to do for us as the man at the pool was doing. When You tell us to take up our mat and walk, may we always listen to You and do what You have told us to do. AMEN.

BREATH OF LIFE

GENESIS 2:7(NIV) *Then the Lord God formed the man of dust from the ground and breathed into his nostrils the breath of life, and man became a living being.*

When God created Adam and Eve, He breathed the breath of life into them, making them living beings. Through this breath of life every one of us lives. During the creation of man and woman, God created the means by which these two would join together and create others. Thus, the human race began.

Upon conception, cells from the mother and father combine and start dividing and re-dividing, creating what will become one of God's most amazing creations. Over the period of gestation, the cells mature into what we can identify as the baby. During this period of time, the baby has all his or her needs met in the warmth of the womb.

At the point of maturity, the baby is ready to leave the mother's womb and enter into a life of his or her own. The baby has been a living being in the womb, but one who is totally dependent upon the mother. I think of how remarkable it is when a newborn baby emerges from the womb and the lifeline to the mother is cut, enabling it to be on its own. I believe that at that moment, God breathes the breath of life into them. One of the first things the baby does is to take oxygen into its lungs and then cry.

As our earthly life comes to an end through age, illness or accident, this breath of life leaves us and we are taken back into the company of God. Our earthly body ceases working and our spiritual self returns to the Creator who first breathed that breath of life into us.

PRAYER: Thank You, God, for breathing that breath of life first into Adam and Eve and from then on into each of us that we can become Your children who worship and praise You for this gift of life. When the time comes for us to return to You, we will breathe our last breath and be with You for eternity. AMEN.

CALLED

ISAIAH 6:8 (NIV) *Then I heard the voice of the Lord saying, "Whom shall I send? And who will go for us?" And I said, "Here am I. Send me!"*

Throughout our lives God calls us to do certain things. It is up to us to listen to that "still, small voice" and answer the call. Some are called to be preachers, teachers, doctors, or other professionals. Sometimes we may hear that call and choose not to answer it. One of my husband's best friends heard the call to full-time professional ministry when he was in college and didn't answer that call until he was in his 50's. Most others don't wait quite that long, but this friend is now in his 70's and still serving our Lord.

After I was divorced, I didn't know how I would support my family and what I would do with my life. At that time, I was in my mid-40's. I had a friend who told me that God had laid it on her heart to tell me I should go to law school. I had worked in the medical field in my first career. I liked the scientific end of that work, and a career in law was about as foreign as I could imagine.

But with that friend's encouragement, I felt that God was calling me into the legal field. After hearing this from her, I checked into the LSAT (Law School Admission Test). The application for the exam was due the next day. I submitted my application and money electronically to get on the list. I found out about a prep class which was starting the next day, and there was one spot left in the class. I saw this as God was working in my life. I took the exam and was admitted to law school.

Upon graduation, I looked for a job and ultimately ended up in private practice in an association of attorneys. I started taking juvenile court appointments as guardian *ad litem* for neglected and abused children. Every time I thought about going in another direction, I would hear that small voice telling me that this was what I was supposed to be doing. After well over 20 years working in the Juvenile Court representing both children and parents of these children, I feel that I did answer God's call.

My greatest acknowledgment that what I was doing was God's calling was when I was presented the Hope Award by one of my former children who had been in foster care. In presenting the award, he stated that I had been there for him at a very pivotal time in his life where he could have gone off in the wrong direction. That award has hung in my office ever since I received it. It states, *"A hundred years from now, it will not matter what my bank account was, the sort of house I lived in, or the kind of car I drove. But the world may be different because I was important in the life of a child."*

We all need to be quiet and listen for that "still, small voice" of God calling us. Who knows where God may lead us or what He will call us to do. We just need to answer with "Here I am, Lord!"

PRAYER: Lord, help us to listen to Your voice and answer Your calls to serve you throughout our lives. Sometimes we fail to answer Your call, but You are a persistent God who never gives up on us and who knows what we are capable of doing and being when we don't know ourselves. Show us Your way and enable us to answer that call with "Here I am, Lord." AMEN.

CHILDREN OF THE LIGHT

JOHN 8:12 (NIV) *When Jesus spoke again to the people, he said, "I am the light of the world. Whoever follows me will never walk in darkness, but will have the light of life."*

B rushy Mountain Penitentiary, where the worst of the worst were sent for over 100 years, is located in East Tennessee. The penitentiary was closed in 2009 and now operates as a tourist attraction. When my husband and I toured this facility, our tour guide was a former inmate. He was incarcerated there for two and a half years of a ten-year sentence, gaining early release for good behavior. As we toured the old penitentiary, he had some stories to tell from his own experience and from those of other inmates. This was not a place you would want to be housed!

There were stories of prisoners being beaten with straps which reminded me of what was done to Jesus in his last hours on this earth. There were other stories of punishments that were inflicted on the prisoners, along with evidence of this in the museum. The worst punishment was being sent to the "hole" for solitary confinement. The "hole" is a cell located in the basement of the laundry room with no access to light. Our guide told us that prisoners sent there lost most of their senses if they were sent there for long periods of time.

Thinking about being sent to the "hole" causes me to consider what total lack of contact with God would be like, what total darkness would be like. The Bible tells us that believers are "children of the light." We walk in the light as we commune with our Lord and Savior. In our homes, there is some form of light coming in even in the middle of the night. We have some light from the moon and stars most nights, from street lights, from electronic equipment in our homes, or we can flip a switch for additional light when needed. Rarely, are we in such a physical state that we don't have some sort of light around. If we are believers, we also have the light of Jesus Christ in our lives. Without that light of Christ, life would be very difficult for most of us to live every day. May His light shine in all our lives!

PRAYER: Jesus, You told us that You were the light of the world and that whomever follows You will never walk in darkness. May we always follow You so that we don't have to live in the "hole" where we are without light and lose all our senses. In Christ name, we pray. AMEN.

CHOICES

2 CORINTHIANS 5:17 (NLT) *This means that anyone who belongs to Christ has become a new person. The old life is gone; a new life has begun!*

If you had your life to live over, what would you do differently? As a group of my friends were discussing this, the end result of our discussion was that we would not change anything. Every choice we have made, good or bad, has helped to mold us into the persons we are today. If you like who you are today, I imagine you will answer it the same way. I'm far from perfect, but I continue to strive to live a life pleasing to God.

As we go through life, we are faced with many choices. Which choice we make determines the direction of our lives. If we make the wrong choice, God gently nudges us back in the direction He wants us to go. Some may resist God's nudging and continue in the wrong direction.

Some have chosen the path of corruption: murder, drugs, and abuse of others. They have each been presented with the choice to turn their lives around and many do, thus creating the person they later become. There are many stories of people finally letting Jesus into their hearts, thus being molded into new persons. If they hadn't had those bad times, they might have never become who they are today. Their testimonies become so powerful that other's lives are changed. Today, Kairos Prison Ministries are growing in many prison systems throughout the United States and abroad. This three-day spiritual retreat is, and continues to be, a pathway to change the lives of many prisoners, male and female, youth and older, into a life of following Jesus Christ. What they have gone through or done in their lives has brought them to where they are today—saved and forgiven.

PRAYER: Lord, no matter what we have done in our lives, we know that You are always there to guide us back onto the life's path that You want us to travel. We always have the choice to alter our path back to following You. AMEN.

FEEDING THE SHEEP

JOHN 10:27 (NLT) *My sheep hear my voice, and I know them, and they follow me.*

On a trip to Norway, we traveled to a working farm and observed a shepherdess feeding the sheep. As we stood and watched, she rang a bell. From all directions, the sheep started coming toward her. The closer she got to us, the more sheep we saw, of all sizes and colors. She had a bucket of bread that she started tossing out to the sheep and then she sat on the ground and fed them. They knew her, and she knew them. We noticed the sheep climbing over each other to get closer to her. As she sat on the ground, they climbed over her to get more of the bread. There were still more of the sheep coming from afar. They knew what the ringing of the bell meant and the reward that she had for them.

Just as the sheep knew their shepherdess and what she had for them, so do we know when we take time to listen to our Good Shepherd. God calls us to His care and has a reward for each of us if we will listen to His beckoning call. He never forsakes any of us and wants to give us the eternal life that He has in store for each of us if we will just listen and answer that call.

The Bible tells of a shepherd leaving 99 sheep to find one that has become lost. So does God come looking for us who have gotten lost in what the world has to offer. We fall victim to many temptations, resulting in our turning from Jesus' teachings. The joy is in having a Lord who loves us and calls us to follow Him just as the shepherdess did with her sheep. We are of many nationalities, cultures, and races, just as her sheep were varied, but God loves and cares for each of us equally. How thankful I am that God loves me just as He loves every one of us!

PRAYER: Lord, keep us close to You just as the shepherd does with his/her sheep. You know each one of us and have known us since our beginning. Let us always follow You and know that if we wander astray, You will come looking for us. AMEN.

FIRE ANTS

MATTHEW 26:33-34 (NIV) *Peter replied, "Even if all fall away on account of you, I never will." "Truly I tell you," Jesus answered, "this very night, before the rooster crows, you will disown me three times."*

Have you ever stepped into a bed of fire ants? Years ago, when I was preparing a flower arrangement for a party, I did. At that time, Queen Ann's Lace was abundant on the roadsides. I pulled off the road with my clippers in hand and wandered into the weeds and wildflowers on the side of the road. Immediately, I felt like my feet were on fire! I couldn't get back to the car fast enough to get my stockings and shoes off. There were hundreds (it seemed) of those pesky little ants crawling all over my feet and legs and stinging me. It seemed like forever before I could brush them all off. My feet immediately swelled to where I couldn't get my shoes back on. At the party, I couldn't get shoes on so I was in stocking feet. Ever since that time, if I am going to trample through weeds and wildflowers off the road, I carefully look where I am stepping.

As we should with our daily lives: look before we leap! How many times in our lives do we aimlessly attack a problem, or just an ordinary task, without checking it out first? We fail to look and see if there is a bed of fire ants right in front of us where our next step is going to be. We often speak before thinking about what we are going to say in certain situations, thus engaging our mouth before our brain.

This reminds me of one of Peter's failures to think before he spoke, especially during those final hours of Jesus' life. Peter told Jesus he'd never deny him, and look what he did. We all need to look before we leap, think before we speak, and check things out before engaging in activities that can be harmful to either ourselves or others.

PRAYER: Lord, help us to stop and think before we act so that we don't end up harming those we know and love, and also those we may not know, but that our actions may end up harming. AMEN.

GOD WILL PROVIDE

MATTHEW 6:26 (NKJV) *Look at the birds of the air; they neither sow nor reap nor gather into barns, and yet your heavenly Father feeds them. Are you not of more value than they?*

As we look out our windows at the birds flying around, we wonder how they know where to look for food. Some dig and eat worms either from the ground or from the tree. Buzzards look for dead animals to eat. God has designed them with different food needs and provides what they need. So it is with all creatures of the earth.

As humans, we also have our needs met by God. He designed us with the ability to provide for ourselves with His leadership. Early people learned how to hunt and gather food to eat from the fields and how to provide clothing and shelter for themselves. As these early people matured in their knowledge, they became more sophisticated in their wants and desires. Now we live in homes made of wood and brick with modern technology that was only a dream in someone's mind a few years ago. God provided the intellect to the inventors and creators of what we use and have today. What a marvelous God who continues to create persons with minds to build and create new technology! We must understand where this comes from and use it for good, not to destroy others.

Sometimes in our lives we are faced with loss of jobs which requires us to look for other work. We even have to re-evaluate our lifestyle, and in some cases, down-size in order to make ends meet. We don't sit at home and expect someone to call and tell us that they have a job for us. We have to do our part in looking for new jobs: pursue leads, apply for jobs, and let others know that we are looking for a new job rather than expecting one to just appear without our participation.

God is always opening doors for us if we will just let him in and follow His lead. He will not desert us even if we desert Him. God's riches are way beyond what we can ever imagine, and God is always there to provide for our needs.

PRAYER: Father, we know that You will always be with us providing for our every need, but at times we need to be nudged to help accomplish that which You are directing us to do. AMEN.

HERE I AM LORD

I SAMUEL 3:8-10 (NKJV): *And the Lord called Samuel again the third time. So, he arose and went to Eli, and said, "Here I am, for you did call me." Then Eli perceived that the Lord had called the boy. Therefore Eli said to Samuel, "Go, lie down; and it shall be, if He calls you, that you must say, 'Speak, Lord, for Your servant hears.'" Samuel went and lay down in his place. Now the Lord came and stood and called as at other times, "Samuel! Samuel!" And Samuel answered, "Speak, for Your servant hears."*

I saw the cutest little dog on TV. His master had decided it was time for a walk, but the doggie didn't want to go, so he flattened himself on the ground with his legs spread out and was flat on his belly being dragged along by his leash. He was so cute resisting his walk.

Thinking of this scene reminded me of the many times that we also resist the call of our Master to do something that we don't want to do. We often use the excuses that we are too busy doing other things, too tired to do the task at hand, and sometimes we just simply don't want to be bothered.

God doesn't call us to do things that are unnecessary or too hard for us to do. He is always there with us to support us in whatever endeavor we are called to do. It may be as simple as making a phone call or as complex as setting up and leading a study group, or caring for a friend or family member. God is always there to support us.

In our scripture reading God called Samuel, but he did not understand it was God calling him until his tutor, the priest Eli, realized who it was. He told Samuel to go lie down and wait to see if God called again. If he did, Samuel was to reply, "Speak, for your servant hears." How many times do we reply to God with those words and follow through with what God wants us to do? One thing I have learned throughout my life is that there is no task too difficult for me if God calls me to it and I respond as Samuel did.

PRAYER: Lord, help us to be more willing to answer in the affirmative when You call us, and to answer as Samuel did, saying, "Speak, for Your servant hears." AMEN.

HOME

JOHN 14:3-4 (NIV) *And if I go and prepare a place for you, I will come back and take you to be with me that you also may be where I am. You know the way to the place where I am going.*

What do you think of when you hear the word home? Home is where I live or reside. Home is where the heart is. Home is where we reside in this earthly life, but it also is where we hope to live for eternity.

Sometimes, we may be in a temporary residence such as away at school, in the military, on a job assignment, in a hospital or long-term facility, or any other place that serves as temporary lodging. When I was away at college, I didn't consider my dorm as home, but as a temporary place where I lived during each semester. Home was where I lived with my parents. I know friends that travel more than they are in the house they own. Home to them is probably wherever they are staying at any given time, or home is where their heart is.

I remember years ago when I was moving from Mississippi back to my home state of Tennessee. I planned to rent my house in Mississippi until I had decided where I would live permanently. The last Sunday I was in my former church our pastor spoke about home being just around the corner. That afternoon, the prospective renters called and wanted my house the following Wednesday. I wasn't planning to leave for several weeks and hadn't packed or made arrangements for the movers. We were both using the same movers and the movers agreed to pack our house the following two days and be able to move the new folks in on Wednesday. We called in friends and neighbors that Sunday and packed and packed even as the movers were carrying things out to the moving van. For the next several weeks our household contents remained loaded on the truck and I lived out of boxes from my car at various friends' homes. At that time home was wherever I was staying for a few days. Finally, the day came for us to travel to Tennessee with our possessions and we had a place to call home again.

Home isn't just a house we live in at this time, but it also is a place we plan to reside in eternity with our Heavenly Father. Jesus told the disciples that He was going away and preparing a place where they would be with Him. We also will be with Him when we leave this earthy home if we accept and believe in our Lord and Savior.

PRAYER: Father, we know that our earthly home is only a temporary residence and that our forever home is with You. Help us never forget where our final residence will be and who it will be with. For this, we give You thanks. AMEN.

HURRY UP AND WAIT

JAMES 5: 7-8 (NIV) *Be patient, then, brothers and sisters, until the Lord's coming. See how the farmer waits for the land to yield its valuable crop, patiently waiting for the autumn and spring rains. You too, be patient and stand firm, because the Lord's coming is near.*

Growing up I had a great aunt who lived with my family. She had raised my mother from her teen years and was the maternal grandmother I never had, since mine died when my mother was ten years old.

Maw Maw, as we called her, was a maiden lady and quite a successful business woman. She had various medical problems over her life requiring frequent doctor visits out of town. She also traveled with her business. Whether it was a doctor's visit or a plane or train she was to catch, she would tell my parents that the appointment was several hours earlier than scheduled. She felt that if she was early, she would be seen earlier. I have never experienced seeing any doctor prior to the appointment time and many times it has been a good deal later that my appointment. Sometimes, Maw Maw would have an appointment at 1:00 and tell us that it was 9 or 10:00. You can imagine what it was like to a young child to have to sit and wait! I don't handle "hurry up and wait" very well, and as a result, I frequently try to get where I am going pretty close to the appointed time.

How often do we spend time sitting and waiting? When we are in the holding pattern of waiting, one way we can use that time is by sitting quietly and communicating with our Heavenly Father regardless of where we may be. I like to make the best use of my time listening to my Father and what He has to say to me. He is always available to me.

I am learning to be patient and to wait for what God has in store for me. It may be sitting, waiting for an appointment, that God places someone in my presence who needs to be heard and to hear encouragement which I should be willing to offer. Waiting is beginning to become more comfortable to me as I learn to listen to God's direction in my life.

PRAYER: Lord, teach us to be patient and listen to what You have to say to us. Don't let us be too busy to follow Your leading. AMEN.

I AM THE DOOR

JOHN 10:9 (NKJV) *I am the door. If anyone enters by Me, he will be saved, and will go in and out and find pasture.*

As we look at the Old and New Testaments, we see many places where doors play an important part in God's plan for this creation. When Noah was instructed to build the ark, those around him treated him like he didn't know what he was doing. Then when the ark was finished and the animals and his family had loaded onto it, God closed and sealed the doors as the rains began. Those who had made fun of Noah tried to enter the ark, but the doors were sealed, closing them out.

Another place the door was important was when the children of Israel were being oppressed by Pharaoh in Egypt. God sent ten plagues in an effort to get Pharaoh to "let my people go." The final plague was the death of all firstborn Egyptian children. In order to distinguish the children of Israel, God told Moses to have them place blood on the door of their homes prior to the angel of death passing over. Herod's firstborn child was one of those killed by the angel of death. The children of Israel were saved by being in their homes and having the blood over their doors. Here the blood over the door protected everyone within. Pharaoh finally let God's people go.

Throughout both the Old and New Testaments, shepherds built barriers around their flocks to prevent other animals from harming their sheep. There was a gate or door into this area. Each sheep knew its shepherd's voice, and the shepherd knew each of his sheep. The shepherd allowed only those he knew and who knew him to enter. So it is with our Good Shepherd. Jesus tells us that He knows each of us by name; and if we know Him and He knows us, we are invited through the door and into His Holy Kingdom to live for eternity. Those who would do harm and do not accept Jesus are not allowed to enter through this door.

PRAYER: May we continue to listen to Your voice when You call us, knowing that if we listen to You and follow You, we will be invited into Your kingdom for eternity. AMEN.

I WALKED WHERE
JESUS WALKED

John 21:15-17 (NIV) *When they had finished eating, Jesus said to Simon Peter, "Simon son of John, do you love me more than these?" "Yes, Lord," he said, "you know that I love you." Jesus said, "Feed my lambs." Again Jesus said, "Simon son of John, do you love me?" He answered, "Yes, Lord, you know that I love you." Jesus said, "Take care of my sheep." The third time he said to him, "Simon son of John, do you love me?" Peter was hurt because Jesus asked him the third time, "Do you love me?" He said, "Lord, you know all things; you know that I love you." Jesus said, "Feed my sheep."*

When we were in the Holy Land, we spent time on and along the Sea of Galilee. As we walked along the coast and crossed the sea in a boat, we read the stories of Jesus choosing the men who would become His disciples: common men, fishermen, a tax collector, a zealot, and others. Of these 12, one of them, Peter, denied Jesus at the most crucial time of Jesus' life, that memorable night right before our Savior was crucified for our sins. Yet he was the one to whom Jesus appeared after his crucifixion and gave the charge to "feed my sheep."

We went to the places where tradition holds that these disciples may have been when called to follow Jesus, where Jesus appeared to Peter and gave him his charge, where the multitudes were fed, where people were healed, where demons were cast out, and where many other of the miracles occurred. We also visited the actual places such as the Sea of Galilee where Jesus walked on water and called Peter to come to him on the water. As we reflect on our trip, look at the photos, and remember the Holy Ground that we walked on, I can't help but think of how the stories of Jesus would play out in our day and time. Think about what each of you would say or do if Jesus wandered through your community and asked you to give up your livelihood and lifestyle to follow him.

We *are* called to be disciples. We believe that Jesus Christ was the Son of God who was crucified for our sins and who on the third day arose and ascended into Heaven to be back with His Father. We are each called to walk where Jesus walked.

As I mentioned, we may not be fishermen as those early disciples were, but we are called to be "fishers of men." We are the chosen ones, the royal priesthood, called to make disciples among our friends, family, neighbors and those we meet through our work, our playtime, our social encounters, and our volunteer endeavors. We are called to be the feet and hands of Jesus to all these people, to help those in need, and to feed those hungry for both physical and spiritual food. We come from different walks of life as did those early disciples, but wherever we may be, we are all the same. It was so good to be with such a caring and loving group of Christian men and women doing what we were called to do and to be. Spending those ten days together walking where Jesus walked so many years ago was the journey of a lifetime.

PRAYER: Father, guide and direct our lives so that we may be "fishers of men" and bring the lost and lonely to You. May we continue to be the hands and feet of Jesus in our daily lives. AMEN.

JESUS STANDS AT THE DOOR AND KNOCKS

REVELATION 3:20 (NKJV) *Behold, I stand at the door and knock; if anyone hears My voice and opens the door, I will come in to him and will dine with him, and he with Me.*

A famous painting shows Jesus standing at a door, knocking. This painting represents Him knocking at the door of our hearts, hoping that we will open that door and let Him into our hearts and lives. He doesn't go away but continues to pursue us. Jesus wants to be part of every one of our lives. Sometimes we make the choice to open that door and sometimes we either ignore the knocking or open the door and then slam it in Jesus' face. No matter what we choose to do, He will always be there waiting for us to make the choice to let Him in. Our Jesus does not give up on us even though we sometimes might give up on Him.

There are people who have turned from God because of drug and alcohol issues, loss of loved ones, illnesses that can't be cured, and natural disasters where the loss of lives was heavy—and thus blamed God. And then there are those bitter and miserable people who choose to believe there is no God.

A man was convicted of murder during a period of time when he was heavily into drugs and had turned from God. One weekend while he was in prison, a Kairos Prison Ministry meeting was being held. With nothing else to do, he attended the meeting. As a result, he opened his heart to Jesus and became a leader inside the prison for the ministry. He has brought many other inmates to Jesus over the years.

If only others would open that door where Jesus is knocking and let Him in, they would enjoy life so much more. I'm not saying that all our aches and pains and disappointments will go away, but we will be better able to cope with them, knowing that Jesus walks along with us. I can't imagine how anyone can deal with the many problems that confront each of us daily without the comfort of His presence.

PRAYER: Jesus, show us the way to reach those who may have turned from You. Enable us to help them open their hearts and minds to You so they may know the love You have for them. May it fill them and overflow to others as it does from all Your followers. AMEN.

KNOWING NOW WHAT
I DIDN'T KNOW THEN

JOHN 13:6-7 (NIV) *He came to Simon Peter, who said to him, "Lord, are you going to wash my feet?" Jesus replied, "You do not realize now what I am doing, but later you will understand."*

At the Last Supper, Jesus prepared to wash the feet of the disciples. When Peter questioned Jesus, His response was profound. He explained that they did not know then what he was doing, but later they would. It took a while for the disciples to understand. We don't know why things happen to us at times, either, but later we realize what it meant.

There's a saying, *"If I only knew then what I know now,"* suggesting that things might have been different, or better, if we had made different decisions. In many cases that's true. Things would have been different, but would that mean they would have been better?

Years ago, my husband moved to California for a career in the music industry, seeking fame and fortune. Looking back now he sees many things he could have done differently that might have led him closer to achieving those early dreams and goals. He frequently comments, "If only I had known then what I know now." Then he adds, "but knowing *now* what I didn't know *then*, I realize things may not have been so good." He knows *now* that he has led a blessed life, one in which God has been directly involved. He knows he has been led in ways that were not necessarily of his own choosing, but in ways that have brought more to his life than he could ever have imagined: family, friends, career, community, love, and so much more are the result of God's leading in his life.

He says he learned about Jesus as a child, and while he may have strayed from time to time, God was always faithful and watching over him. Looking back, he sees where God knew more about what was best, and he's grateful for the path his life took, knowing now what he didn't know then.

PRAYER: Lord, You know more about what is good and the right direction for our lives. Help us to follow Your leading rather than our own desires. Only You know what is best for us. AMEN.

LEARNING TO SWIM

JOHN 14:6-7 (NKJV) *Jesus said to him: "I am the way, the truth and the life. No one comes to the Father except through me. If you had known Me, you would have known My Father also; and from now on you know Him and have seen Him."*

On my first day of swim lessons, a classmate threw me into the deep end of the pool. I was scared and the life-guard had to get me out and resuscitate me. I did learn to swim eventually. However, the fear of water has remained with me.

At whatever age we learn to swim, it is a process. Each step is necessary. First, we must become comfortable in the water as we slowly enter the pool. The next step is to learn to hold our breath under water. Then, we move to learning to float on our backs and then on our stomachs. Generally, an instructor is there to support our bodies until they can remove their support and we can float on our own. Gradually we learn to use our arms and legs to move through the water. All the time there is someone alongside us to provide support and encouragement in order to remove the fear of water. I am convinced that God sends His angels to us in our time of need. These angels may be in the form of a lifeguard, doctor, pastor, neighbor, friend, or a total stranger.

Every day we face challenges. When we are unable to deal with them *alone,* we need someone to rely on. Those who believe in Jesus as their Savior can face these challenges successfully. We should always be open to God's intervention in our lives to rescue us from the dangers that are present and those that lie ahead of us.

God has already sent His Son to show us the Way. Christ is the truth and the light of the world. All we have to do is be open to His love and accept Him as our Lord and Savior.

PRAYER: God, may we always be open to You and those You send to help us in our time of need. We know that You will never leave nor forsake us. AMEN.

LIGHT

John 8:12 (NIV) *Again Jesus spoke to them, saying, "I am the light of the world. Whoever follows me will not walk in darkness, but will have the light of life."*

During the day we have light from the sun, and at night we have light from the moon. We light our homes with various types of fixtures, enabling us to move freely about. We live in a society where light is part of our lives. In other parts of the world, there are places where the *only* light is that which comes from the sun or moon.

Sailors at sea rely upon the sun, moon, and stars for their travels. When they are close to shore, lighthouses guide them when there is not enough light from the sun or moon to navigate dangerous places or shorelines. Pilots of airplanes use runway lights to guide them when they take off and land. Towers and other indicators flash to notify the pilots of dangers ahead which they might otherwise fly into. Light is something we all relate to.

Jesus said that He is the "light of the world." He tells us that whoever follows Him will not walk in darkness. With Jesus as our light, we see dangers ahead and do all we can to avoid wrong turns and obstacles that might harm us. Sometimes we turn off our Jesus light and wander in darkness again, but He is faithful to recue us so we can continue to walk in the light, read and study the Bible, and tell others about Him.

PRAYER: Jesus, help us to always keep Your light burning in our hearts so that we may avoid the obstacles that may clutter our way. Without Your light in our lives, we become lost and make the wrong choices in life. Let us always be mindful that You are the Light of the World. AMEN.

LIKE A LITTLE CHILD

MARK 10:13-16 (NIV) *People were bringing little children to Jesus for him to place his hands on them, but the disciples rebuked them. When Jesus saw this, he was indignant. He said to them, "Let the little children come to me, and do not hinder them, for the kingdom of God belongs to such as these. Truly I tell you, anyone who will not receive the kingdom of God like a little child will never enter it." And he took the children in his arms, placed his hands on them and blessed them.*

Jesus tells us that we need to receive the kingdom of God like a little child. Children are trusting, loving, and forgiving. Receiving the kingdom as a child doesn't mean to be young in age, but like a little child: trusting, loving and forgiving. You can be any age when you accept Jesus

The opportunity is always there for each of us throughout our lives, but Some people wait until they are old or on their deathbed to accept Jesus as their Lord and Savior. I think of all the joys of life they have missed out on by not having Him as a part of their lives until the very end.

Just as children hold onto their parents' hands when crossing the street or walking down the sidewalk, so does Jesus hold our hands as we walk life's path. Mothers comfort us when we need comforting regardless of our age and so does Jesus. We are always our parents' children whatever age we may be and so it is with Jesus.

PRAYER: Lord, as we grow older in our physical bodies, may we continue to be like little children, open to learning more about You every day, growing deeper in our faith. AMEN.

NEEDS V. WANTS

PHILIPPIANS 4:19 (NIV) *And my God will meet all your needs according to the riches of his glory in Christ Jesus.*

How often do we see or hear of things and decide we want them no matter the cost: physical, emotional, financial, or spiritual? In such situations our question should be, "Do I really need this?" Considering needs versus wants has been a challenge for most of us.

Often, fulfilling a want can end up costing much more than just the financial expense of the item. Look at the news and read the newspapers to see where people get so caught up in the wants that they end up breaking the law, ending up incarcerated. The selfish desire to have something we can't legally have frequently causes the loss of families, friends, jobs, and homes. Is it really worth it to have things obtained illegally or fraudulently?

Most of us do not go to the extremes described above, but sometimes we do let our wants supersede our needs, and we end up bringing a financial burden on either ourselves or our families. We need to step back and assess what is really important.

God tells us that He will provide for our needs. Our basic needs are food, clothing, and shelter. There are many people of the world, even in our own communities, who do not have these needs met. However, there are many agencies and groups who work to provide for those in need. They act as the hands and feet of God, providing for the needy.

As I grew up, there were many times that a friend or her family had something that I thought I wanted. My parents provided well for me, but not all of my wants were met. I never went without any of the basics, just some of my wants. I learned a valuable lesson in this act of love from my parents: I learned that just because I wanted something it didn't mean that I always got it. Sometimes I would get it later on, and then other times, not at all. Often, I found that I really didn't need it or that it would have been bad for me to have. I wonder what kind of person I would be today if I had gotten everything I wanted. There would be no appreciation for what I have now.

PRAYER: Lord, help us to determine the difference in wants and needs. We know that You provide for our needs; it is our job to be satisfied with what we have and not look at what others have and be envious of them. AMEN.

NOTE ON THE
KITCHEN TABLE

MATTHEW 11:25 (NIV) *At that time Jesus said, "I praise you, Father, Lord of heaven and earth, because you have hidden these things from the wise and learned, and revealed them to little children.*

After going through a difficult divorce, I did not know what the future had in store for me. I had many friends who supported me through this difficult time. My older son was a senior in high school, and I knew that I couldn't make any changes that would affect his relationship with his school friends. Many of them had been in school with him since pre-school, had played sports with him, and gone to church with him throughout his life.

I had not worked since having children. I knew that I had to pursue a new career. If I went back to work in my former medical job, I would have to work for my former husband, which was not an acceptable option. I prayed constantly for God to leave me a note on the kitchen table as to what He had in store for my future. During my marriage, my husband and I frequently left notes on the kitchen table regarding what was going on for the day. I wanted God to just write me a note, although I knew that was not going to happen.

In January, prior to my son's graduation, we were playing cards together. Abruptly and with no prompting, he said, "Momma, I think you should move back to Tennessee where Nana and your brother live." He went on to say that he would be attending school at Vanderbilt and that it would be nice for us to be close by, but he didn't want me to do anything until after his graduation in May. I started crying, grabbed him, and hugged him. Rather than a note on the kitchen table, God spoke to me through my 18-year-old son! I told him that I had been praying for a direction and he had provided it! This was one of the options I had pondered over that last year or so, but hearing it from my son made it real. After further discussion, the boys got boxes and started packing their things even though it was several months before graduation and the time we would move.

I contacted friends in Tennessee and traveled there with my younger son to find a place to live. After graduation, we packed up and away we went! I have never looked back. God did put a note on the kitchen table, but it came through my son's voice rather than on a piece of paper.

PRAYER: Let us always be open to answers to our prayers which frequently come when and how we least expect them. You choose how to respond to us in Your own way and we need to keep our eyes and ears open to those answers. Thank You for always taking care of us. In Jesus' name we pray. AMEN.

ONE BODY

I CORINTHIANS 12:12 (NIV) *Just as a body, though one, has many parts, but all its many parts from one body, so it is with Christ.*

I live in a retirement community where the average age is probably somewhere around 75-80. Taking this into consideration, you can imagine that we are a unique church congregation. We have only an occasional baptism, which is generally a grandchild or great-grandchild of one of our congregants, and few weddings. We instead have far more memorial services than an average congregation.

Although we are of retirement age, it doesn't mean that we aren't involved in serving our Lord and Savior. We collectively are from all walks of life and share the various gifts that we have been given with others in our church family and community. We now have time to give of ourselves more than when we were working full-time and in most cases raising children, which consumed most of our free time. We have time now for recreational and cultural events; we also have time to volunteer within our church and the community; and time to study the Bible through classes offered during the week.

I have realized that it takes people of all backgrounds, educational levels, careers, and family histories to come together to make a church. We have all been given different gifts to offer to others and it takes all of these gifts to make the family of God whole. We have in our church family educators, medical professionals, lawyers and judges, retired military, people from the manufacturing field, carpenters, engineers, many retired clergy, and members from various other walks of life. Each one, regardless of past career, has something to offer and share with one another, to support one another in time of need and strengthen our congregation in helping one another to be the people of God that He wants us to be.

The hymn "We Are the Church" tells me that "I am the church, you are the church, we are the church together..." We the people are the church. The church is not merely a building that we go to for worship and fellowship. It is a gathering place for the children of God to worship and praise Him, pray, thank Jesus, share communion, and grow our faith through study of His Word. The church is one body, we the people.

PRAYER: Thank You, God, for bringing the people of our churches together to worship, pray and praise You as well as to serve You. No matter what our backgrounds are we all have something to offer and together we will become one body in service to You. AMEN.

OWNERSHIP

PROVERBS 23:3-4 (NIV) *By wisdom a house is built, and through understanding it is established; through knowledge its rooms are filled with rare and beautiful treasures.*

In 1976, Millard and Linda Fuller began Habitat for Humanity to provide homes for those who could not financially afford one. Through Habitat for Humanity, lives have been changed and communities have been built throughout the world. Today, Habitat operates in all 50 states and in over 90 countries.

I wonder if the Fullers ever imagined what a difference they would make to so many families and communities worldwide. Prospective recipients must put 500 hours of "sweat equity" into building other Habitat homes and then their own home. Having recipients put sweat equity into their home gives them a sense of ownership. They weren't just given ownership of a home, they worked for it and put their own energy into making their dream come true. Don't you cherish the things that you worked for more than those that were just given to you?

God's love is different. His love is there waiting for each of us to claim. We don't have to work for it. He gives it to us freely, but we must be willing to ask for it and accept it when given. He forgives us when we go astray, but again we must ask for forgiveness and then we will receive it, freely.

PRAYER: Lord, help us ask for assistance when we are in need and help us realize that this is the beginning of our relationship with You. "Asking and accepting" is "the work" that we do to receive the love, mercy and grace that is so freely given. AMEN.

PLANS I HAVE FOR YOU

JEREMIAH 29:11 (NIV) *"For I know the plans I have for you," declares the Lord, "plans to prosper you and not to harm you, plans to give you hope and a future."*

As I go through life, the knowledge that God has a plan for me gives me strength and hope for tomorrow. I am sure that many of you feel the same way. I think of those who do not believe God has a plan for them, who therefore go aimlessly along their way, not knowing which way to turn at any time. The hopelessness they must feel! This is not to say that those of us who believe God has a plan for us will know what the plan is until it happens, but we do know and believe that God's plan is to "prosper us and not to harm us." What a comfort that is!

Today, there are more and more people taking anti-depressants and self-medicating with drugs and alcohol than ever before. Many have chemical imbalances which require anti-depressants; I personally have known some of them. There are others who gave up on being happy because of circumstances beyond their control who then returned to their faith and the knowledge that God created them and is always there to get them through tough times. These people seem to be the happiest and most grateful that they have a Lord and Savior who loves them unconditionally and wants them to prosper no matter what is going on around them. We face nothing in this life that God can't help us walk through. Even when we are facing death, He is there welcoming us into the company of saints in Heaven. God carries us to be with Him in eternal life. All we have to do is accept forgiveness for our sins that Jesus took to the cross with Him, and believe!

PRAYER: Lord, may we always remember that You are there to care for us no matter what the circumstances. Help us not to fall into a life of loneliness or unhappiness where we revert to unhealthy means of seeking happiness that only You can provide. You are always ready to welcome us into Your open arms and comfort us. AMEN.

POTTER'S WHEEL

ISAIAH 64:8 (NKJV) *But now, O LORD, You are our Father; We are the clay, and You our potter; And all we are the work of Your hand.*

As a potter, I can relate to this scripture. The first task the potter faces is to decide what to create in order to know how much clay to use. Then he or she takes a block of raw clay and works with it until it is pliable and can be placed upon a potter's wheel. The ball must be evenly round and laid on the center of the wheel. The potter starts working with the clay, careful to keep the ball perfectly centered. The speed of the wheel is important. If the potter spins too fast, the clay will fly off the wheel.

Once the clay ball is uniform and centered the potter starts creating, using slow and decisive movements, shaping a vessel. When finished, it is carefully removed from the wheel, trimmed, and allowed to completely dry. Then it is placed inside a kiln for the first firing. After the first firing it is cooled, glazed, re-fired and cooled again. Finally, the vessel is fit for service.

God is the potter; we are the clay. He works gently and decisively to form us into the person we are meant to be. We have free will to respond to God's leading us. He wants to mold us and make us into a serving vessel, but we have to submit to His shaping work. As we remain centered in God's guidance, He makes something beautiful and useful out of each of us.

PRAYER: Lord, as You mold each of us into the unique vessel we were intended to be, help us to be willing to submit to Your shaping of our lives into that which You want us to become. AMEN.

REJECTION

LUKE 10:16 (NLT) *Then he said to the disciples, "Anyone who accepts your message is also accepting me. And anyone who rejects you is rejecting me. And anyone who rejects me is rejecting God, who sent me."*

We remember that Jesus was rejected even by his own hometown and others along the way. He ended up being persecuted and beaten then experienced the most devastating death—death on a cross. The Romans and Jewish leaders intended to put an end to His preaching and teaching, but this was not the end for Him, only the beginning. On Easter Sunday, Jesus was resurrected and later ascended back to His Father where He lives even today. This was not the end that was envisioned by those who did not believe his teaching. Many who witnessed these events had their eyes opened that day and in the days to come.

Have you ever felt rejected—feeling that no one was listening to you—that you weren't part of the group? I have come to believe that all of us have had a feeling of rejection at some point in our lives. It is what we decide to do with our feelings that matters. Do we retaliate and attack those who are rejecting us or just walk away hurting? Each situation must be taken individually. Sometimes it is best to confront the rejection and try to see where the other person is coming from. You may be able to come to an amicable resolution; other times, it is better to just walk away. Those rejecting you may not be rejecting you as a person. It could be the ideas you are presenting that they don't like, not you.

Remember you are not the only one who has ever been rejected. If the Romans and Jews and even Jesus' own hometown rejected the Son of God, should you feel above rejection? More importantly, do you practice rejecting others, even God's own Son?

PRAYER: Lord, help us to deal with rejection when we are faced with it. You know the sting of rejection and are able to guide and direct us when we feel it. May we never choose to reject You. AMEN.

SEA OF GALILEE

MARK 4:35-40 (NLT) *As evening came, Jesus said to his disciples, "Let's cross to the other side of the lake." So they took Jesus in the boat and started out, leaving the crowds behind (although other boats followed). But soon a fierce storm came up. High waves were breaking into the boat, and it began to fill with water. Jesus was sleeping at the back of the boat with his head on a cushion. The disciples woke him up, shouting, "Teacher, don't you care that we're going to drown?" When Jesus woke up, he rebuked the wind and said to the waves, "Silence! Be still!" Suddenly the wind stopped, and there was a great calm. Then he asked them, "Why are you afraid? Do you still have no faith?" The disciples were absolutely terrified. "Who is this man?" they asked each other. "Even the wind and waves obey him!"*

Several years ago, we were privileged to travel to the Holy Land and experience places where Jesus and his disciples walked, preached, and lived. Upon arriving we were taken to a kibbutz located on the shore of the Sea of Galilee. The first day there, we went out on the sea, dropped anchor, and shared scriptures relating to Jesus calming the sea. The water was still and looked like a sheet of glass beneath us. It was hard to visualize the storm that is described by Mark. Early the next morning, we heard trees blowing about, some of their branches brushing the outside of our cottage. in the distance, the sea was white capping. A storm like the disciples experienced had arrived. No boats were allowed on the water that day. We gave thanks that for our trip on the sea we had calm, smooth water. We were told that the Sea of Galilee is the lowest freshwater lake on the Earth and second lowest overall (behind the Dead Sea, which is a saltwater lake). With mountains surrounding the sea, winds can come in unexpectedly causing sudden tumultuous storms on the water. This information gives us a better understanding of the story told in Mark's gospel.

When the storm came upon the disciples, they were so afraid they called out to Jesus for help. When we face life's storms, we can also reach out to Jesus to calm the raging storms in our lives. One day life is smooth like the water on the Sea of Galilee and the next day a storm blows in and engulfs us. It could be a diagnosis of health issues outside our control; a phone call from a family member or friend that a loved one has died or is ill; a tragedy in the news that affects us deeply and personally. Life is never the same after such storms arise, but we can take comfort in knowing that Jesus is with us throughout them. He will walk with us, carry us, comfort us, and answer our prayers when we turn to Him. Our prayers may not always be answered in the ways we think they should be, but we can rely on the assurance that God's will *will* be done in our lives.

PRAYER: Thank You, Lord, for being with us whatever circumstances we may be facing. Let us hear Your voice as You calm the raging seas in our lives. AMEN.

STAGES OF LOVE

1 JOHN 4:17 (NLT) *And as we live in God, our love grows more perfect. So we will not be afraid on the day of judgment, but we can face him with confidence because we live like Jesus here in this world.*

As we grow from babies to adults, we experience the growth of love—how we receive it and how we give it. A newborn baby is totally dependent upon its parents or care giver to learn about love. Almost immediately parents begin to cuddle their baby. We talk "baby talk" and as they feel the love we express to them, they respond by cooing and smiling early on. They cry when they need something or when something hurts, unable to express their needs in any other way. We learn what that cry means by trial and error. As they learn to crawl and walk, they stay right by our sides, receiving the love we have for them and reciprocating as they learn how.

As children grow, their expressions of love may vary from child to child. Even in abusive settings, children long for love and acceptance from the abusive parent. There is a bond there regardless of the treatment they may receive.

During teenage years, children start learning a different kind of love than what they have developed with their parents and other family members. They start becoming attracted to the opposite sex and experience their first expressions of puppy love. Some of these early infatuations may end up in a lifetime relationship through marriage.

The love they feel on their wedding day grows into something very special as they choose to live out their lives together. Some celebrate 50-60 years of love and marriage after feeding and nurturing their love for each other. The important part here is that they nurture and feed their love so it may grow.

In the same way, we need to nurture our relationship with our Lord and Savior. The closer we grow toward God, the more perfect our love becomes. God loves us unconditionally, and if we don't stay connected with Him, it is we who suffer the loss of a relationship. He will never turn His back on us. He is always there!

PRAYER: Teach us how to love each other more every day as we grow closer to that perfect love that You have for us. May our love spread to those with whom we come in contact, so they may feel Your love for them. AMEN.

STILL SMALL VOICE

JOHN 14:16-18 (NIV) *And I will ask the Father, and he will give you another advocate to help you and be with you forever – the Spirit of truth. The world cannot accept him, because it neither sees him nor knows him. But you know him, for he lives with you and will be in you. I will not leave you as orphans; I will come to you.*

When you are trying to make a decision, do you always ask God to direct you and follow His leading? If so, do you hear that still small voice inside you telling you which way to go? When you don't ask for God's direction and go blindly into something, do you have the feeling that something is wrong? As I meditate on these questions, I can remember many times when I didn't ask God for direction and made my own decision. I worried about that decision, lay awake at night wishing I had made a different choice, and finally, I went to God in prayer asking for direction dealing with the issue at hand. There were other times when I prayed about issues and followed the direction that the voice inside led me to make. I didn't worry about what I had decided. I didn't lay awake at night worrying about it. I had peace within myself about the decision I had made.

Many years ago, my husband and I were visiting where we currently live and were taken around the area to look at homes and lots. We were many years from retirement and we weren't looking to buy or build for a while. When we saw our current lot, I looked at him and said, "I'm going to buy this lot for us to retire here someday." Where did that come from? We prayed about the decision and I closed on the property that day. I know God had plans for us then and I have never doubted that decision. It was another 13-14 years before we saw that dream come to fruition.

I had listened to that voice inside me leading us to this place. I never doubted the decision because I knew that it was what God wanted for us.

We live in a lovely community, have made many new friends, and have never been happier.

PRAYER: Help us to listen to what You have to say to us and follow Your directions. May we take time to be still and listen to that small voice as You direct our lives. AMEN.

THE DASH

PSALM 139:16 (NLT) *You saw me before I was born. Every day of my life was recorded in your book. Every moment was laid out before a single day had passed.*

On tombstones, between the date we are born and the date we die, there is a dash. That dash encompasses our lives and what we did from the first day to the last day of life. Did you ever stop and think about what is included in the "dash"? For some people that dash represents a long time and for others a short time. But for all of us there is a dash.

When we are born, our parents take care of us providing food, clothing, and shelter. As we grow, we are taught right from wrong. For those of us who are brought up in a Christian family, we are taught about Jesus and his wondrous love—though many don't have that Christian upbringing. As we grow older, we begin to make our own choices in life. Some of these choices may determine how long or short the dash may represent.

God alone knows how many years we will live. He told us in Psalm 139:16 that He knew us before we were even formed. Again, Ecclesiastes 7:17 warns us to "not be overly wicked, nor be foolish so that we may die before our time." There are many circumstances that we may face during our lifetime that will determine how long that dash represents. God does not cause us to experience disease and accidents. Sometimes they are a result of choices we have made. Remember that God gave us free will. The warning from Ecclesiastes tells us not to be wicked or foolish. We need to live a life that is pleasing to God and remember that He is always with us no matter what our circumstances may be.

I still wonder why some people live only a short time and others live into their 90's and even reach 100 plus. This is not a question any of us can answer. But if we are God's people, He has plans for us that we cannot know. Simply live in a manner that pleases God and He will take care of everything else.

PRAYER: God, help me to live the kind of life You have in store for me. May the time the dash represents be pleasing to You. AMEN.

THEY WILL KNOW WE
ARE CHRISTIANS

JOHN 13:34-35 (NIV) *"A new command I give you: Love one another. As I have loved you, so you must love one another. By this everyone will know that you are my disciples, if you love one another."*

At the Last Supper Jesus knew that the time had come for His departure from this earth, but He was still teaching the disciples, and us as well, with the familiar verses above. Today, people will know that we are Christians by our love. We do not have to go out on the street corners and profess our beliefs nor do we have to take out ads in the newspapers or get on television to tell others that we are Christians. They will see who we are by the way we live, by the way we love others, care for others, treat others, and the way we speak to others.

Many people may claim to be Christians, but when you look closely at the way they live and treat others, you may question their sincerity. I am careful not to be too judgmental for only God knows who they really are. We frequently see on the news those who claim to be Christians disrespecting others; people who are not like them, or don't think like them. Yet they still claim to be Christians. Do they really love their brothers and sisters? I can't answer that question, but by their actions, it doesn't seem like they do.

As an attorney, I frequently would see people coming into court with their Bible in hand and making a point of sitting and reading it. My cynical mind would notice that most of the time the Bibles they carried appeared to be brand new. I assume they were trying to impress a judge that they were Christian by carrying their Bible with them to court. I am reminded of Matthew 6:1 where Jesus is teaching us not to practice our righteous acts in front of others, for if we do, we will have no reward from our Father in heaven.

On the other hand, I have been surprised when someone I do not know tells me they know I am a Christian by how I act and treat others.

This is what Jesus was teaching throughout his ministry. We need to learn to love unselfishly as Jesus did so others will know we are Christians.

PRAYER: May my actions and words be pleasing to You, O God, so that others coming in contact with me will know I am a Christian. Guard my heart and mouth so that I don't say or do something that would be harmful to those around me. AMEN.

THREE IN ONE

GENESIS 1:26 (NIV) *And God said, Let us make man in our image, after our likeness; and let them have dominion over the fish of the sea, and over the fowl of the air, and over the cattle, and over all the earth, and over every creeping thing that creepeth upon the earth.*

One of the most difficult concepts for me to understand as a child was how God was the Father, the Son, and the Holy Spirit all wrapped up in one. I remember in school we were taught that several elements come in different forms according primarily to the temperature. Water can be ice when frozen, liquid when thawed, and vapor when heated. Regardless of what form it is in, water is water, or H2O. That explained a little more how God could be three beings, all at the same time.

I learned that in the beginning God spoke and the earth and all things above and below the surface along with all living things were created. He had an organized plan as to what came first. There had to be somewhere for man to ultimately live, so he created the heavens and the earth, then day and night, plants and animals for man to use to eat, and a perfect place for him to live. Finally, He created man. If he had created man before all these other things, what good would it have been to have a living human without a place to live or sustenance to support him?

Now I know that all three beings of the God-head were in place in the beginning, since the scriptures state that God said, "Let us create man *in our image*" (emphasis added). When things on earth were not going well, God the Father decided to send Jesus, the Son, to be a human example to show mankind the way He wanted us to live. After Jesus left the world, God the Father sent an advocate in the form of the Holy Spirit to live within us and continue to guide and teach us. Thus, we can think of God as unimaginable, God in human form as Jesus, and God the Holy Spirit as invisible within us.

PRAYER: God, thank You, for Your creation of this world and everything in it and then for creating mankind in Your image. May we never forget that You are the Father, Son, and Holy Spirit all wrapped into one. AMEN.

UNEXPECTED GIFTS FROM UNLIKELY PEOPLE

I CORINTHIANS 1:26-29 (NIV) *Brothers and sisters, think of what you were when you were called. Not many of you were wise by human standards; not many were influential; not many were of noble birth. But God chose the foolish things of the world to shame the wise; God chose the weak things of the world to shame the strong. God chose the lowly things of this world and the despised things—and the things that are not—to nullify the things that are, so that no one may boast before him.*

As we look at both the Old and New Testaments, we see how God chose unlikely people to carry out his mission for this world. Today, He is still choosing unlikely people to carry out unexpected tasks.

One of those in the Old Testament was Moses, who was called to lead the children of Israel out of Egypt to the Promised Land. In the New Testament one was Mary, a peasant girl God called to be the mother of Jesus. Paul, another unlikely person, was one of the Pharisees dedicated to persecuting the early Christians. He was on the road to Damascus when Jesus appeared to him and he became one of the leaders in the early Christian church. Not to be forgotten are those who were called to be the disciples, like a fisherman and a tax collector.

Today God is still calling unlikely persons to do unexpected things. Those who have experienced life-threatening diseases have gone on to form research foundations. One of these is Kathi Giusti, who after being diagnosed with multiple myeloma, founded the Multiple Myeloma Research Foundation. Susan Komen's sister founded Susan G. Komen for the Cure to promote breast cancer education and research after losing Susan to breast cancer. Charles Colson, who was involved in the Watergate coverup, went on to form Prison Fellowship after his incarceration. Former President of the United States Jimmy Carter became a worker with Habitat for Humanity, where he has been involved since the end of his presidency.

You may be called out of your ordinary life to do extraordinary acts. God is still calling ordinary persons to do extraordinary things. They succeed when they follow where God leads. Who knows what God has in store for those who listen and follow?

PRAYER: May we always be open to Your calling in our lives. Help us to answer that calling for we don't know what You see in us or why You chose us when You call us to do Your work here on earth. AMEN.

VISIONS

JEREMIAH 29:11(NIV) *"... For I know the plans I have for you," declares the LORD, "plans to prosper you and not to harm you, plans to give you hope and a future..."*

Throughout the Bible, there are examples of God giving his people visions. Jacob had a vision of a ladder leading to Heaven. Joseph interpreted visions for the Pharaoh. John had a vision of Heaven. The most amazing was the vision God gave Noah of how to build the Ark.

Several years ago, we visited The Ark Encounter in Kentucky. The creator of the Ark Encounter must also have had a vision in creating this exhibit. The dimensions, as recorded in Genesis, were followed as closely as possible. To show how all the animals and Noah's family lived on the Ark, creativity may have taken place in construction, but it is my belief that it was a vision from God.

I believe that God continues to give visions to his people. Visions to create memorials of events of our history, visions of creating service programs for those in need, and man-made wonders of the world. Memorials to lives lost in so many of this country's wars are displayed in Washington, DC. In New York and at the Pentagon, memorials have clearly been visions of meaningful ways to celebrate those lives lost during 9/11. They serve as a lasting memory of what has happened in our country's history so that we never forget them or repeat them. God continues to give us visions today.

PRAYER: Heavenly Father, help us to be open to visions You may have for us. Let these visions help us to remember events that have happened so that we do not forget all You have created for us. AMEN.

WE ARE ALL GOD'S PEOPLE

GENESIS 11:6-9 (NIV) *The LORD said, "If as one people speaking the same language they have begun to do this, then nothing they plan to do will be impossible for them. Come, let us go down and confuse their language so they will not understand each other." So, the LORD scattered them from there over all the earth, and they stopped building the city. That is why it was called Babel —because there the LORD confused the language of the whole world. From there the LORD scattered them over the face of the whole earth.*

Years ago, when traveling internationally, I was in a major airport where planes from all over the world terminated flights. The queues for the passengers to go through immigration and customs were packed with deplaning passengers. I noticed people from many nationalities and races. Many of these persons were in their native dress, and all were speaking languages I did not recognize. I don't remember ever being a part of such a diverse group of people. I have traveled various places since, but that gathering of people is the largest I have ever seen or been a part of. It reminded me of the time when God confused the language of the whole world and scattered the people over the face of the earth.

In the Genesis story, everyone spoke the same language. But the people got themselves in trouble with God when they decided to build a tower to the heavens in order to make a name for themselves. God intervened to give them different languages and to scatter them over the face of the earth. Today, there is no way of counting the various languages and dialects of the world. Even so, God knows each of us regardless of where we live or what our customs, dress, or languages are. We are all God's people, and He loves each of us equally no matter where we live or what language we speak.

PRAYER: Help us to remember that even though we come from all over the world, speak different languages, and have different customs, we are all Your children. We still know You and call You "Father." AMEN.

WHERE GOD LEADS ME

MATTHEW 4:18-19 (NIV) *As Jesus was walking beside the Sea of Galilee, he saw two brothers, Simon called Peter and his brother Andrew. They were casting a net into the lake, for they were fishermen. "Come, follow me," Jesus said, "and I will send you out to fish for people."*

God speaks to us in a "still small voice" saying, "Follow Me." How often do we sit still and listen to what God has in store for us and is calling us to do?

Quite a few years ago, my husband's employer closed the business where he worked. We did not know what he was going to do since he was not old enough to retire and we needed his income. After much job hunting and prayer, he received a call from our senior pastor asking him to join the staff at our church as Director of Single Adult Ministry. My husband and I had met years previously in the singles' program at that church and then married. He knew the needs of single adults, having been part of this group for many years. After thinking about it and praying about it, we decided this was the right place and time for him to pursue this work. I supported him, and the activities of this ministry became our social and spiritual life. We both believed that God had called him to this ministry. He felt that God had been preparing him for this job for many years, and it turned out to be the most fulfilling job he ever held.

Years after retiring, once again he received a call from our senior pastor asking him to join the staff at our new church as part-time Director of Assimilation and Hospitality. Again, we prayed about it, and he held that position for several years. He really loved what he was doing and felt called once again to serve the Lord.

How many times do we answer the call to follow Jesus and serve Him wherever it may be? Living in a retirement community, we see some called to serve helping the homeless, or the sick and suffering, through caring ministries. Some work with children who need mentoring or need clothing or food, and some volunteer through many other ministries and organizations in our community. Regardless of age God continues to call us to serve. Listen to hear where Jesus is calling you to serve, and follow His invitation to help those around you who need to know His love.

PRAYER: Father, may we continually listen to that still small voice as You call us into service. We should remember that when You call, You know that we can do the job, so help us to answer yes, knowing that we can do anything with Your support. AMEN.

SPECIAL
DAYS

CHANGES

HEBREWS 13:8 (NIV) *Jesus Christ is the same yesterday and today and forever.*

As we look around our community we see many changes, from the weather to the seasonal change of plant life, to new construction. As we look around our church community, we see many changes as well. We have lost friends through death and others who have moved away to be closer to family in their later years of life. There are those whose health has caused them to have to change their lifestyle as well. We have all grown older and some of our "parts" don't work as well as they did in our younger years. Everywhere we look, we can see and experience changes. This is all part of God's plan.

I remember the movie *Groundhog Day* and think how boring it would be without the changes we all experience every day. I look forward to each new day and wonder what new experiences God has in store for me. What a joy each day will be if we all keep that in mind!

As we approach the Lenten season in our church, I think about the changes the disciples and early followers of Jesus had after the death and resurrection of our Lord and Savior. There were amazing changes in store for those early Christians. They had lost their leader and teacher. They were then commissioned to bring the Word of God to all peoples, sharing Jesus' teachings with those they came in contact with, thus beginning the early church. Without the indwelling of the Holy Spirit, they could not have carried out this mission. We too, in spite of all the changes we see around us, have a mission to carry out—to spread the Good News of Jesus' life, death, and resurrection to all those we meet. We must remember that there is one thing that will never change: the love God has for every one of us. It is the only constant in our lives!

PRAYER: We give thanks for the love You have for each of Your children. Be with us and encourage us to continue spreading Your Word to a world that desperately needs to hear it. We face changes every day of our lives, but You never change—You are our constant! AMEN.

THIRTY PIECES
OF SILVER

MATTHEW 26:14 (NKJV) *Then one of the twelve, called Judas Iscariot, went to the chief priests and said, "What are you willing to give me if I deliver Him to you?" And they counted out to him thirty pieces of silver.*

During Holy Week, we read about that final week of Jesus' life: Palm Sunday, Jesus' triumphal entry into Jerusalem and then as the week unfolded, we faced Judas' betrayal of Jesus, all for thirty pieces of silver! You may wonder what the thirty pieces of silver were worth. Exodus 21:32 tells us that thirty pieces of silver was the value of a slave. In essence, it was an insult to pay this amount to Judas to identify Jesus. Jesus had been among the priests and pharisees since the beginning of his ministry and they should have known who he was without Judas giving him a kiss. I wonder why Judas went to them offering to betray Jesus and turn him over to them. My belief is that Satan had entered into him and he succumbed to Satan. Matthew 27:5 tells us that Judas then went out and hanged himself.

We too are tempted by Satan every day. He wants us to follow him rather than our Lord and Savior. Many people give in to Satan and then find out that what he promised did not come true and they are then stuck with their decisions. There have been several books and movies depicting people selling their souls to Satan and then regretting it.

In the gospels, we read about Satan tempting Jesus by trying to get Him to buy into Satan's false promises. After being baptized by John, Jesus went into the wilderness for 40 days and nights to fast. There Satan appeared to Jesus and tempted Him three times. First, Satan tempted Jesus by commanding Him to turn stones to bread; then he took Jesus to the pinnacle of the temple and told Him to throw Himself down and let the angels take care of Him; the third temptation was when Satan took him to a high mountain and told Jesus that if He would worship Satan, that all this would be his. Jesus replied as follows in Matthew 4:10, "Away with you, Satan! For it is written, you shall worship the Lord your God, and Him only you shall serve."

We are all sinners and face these temptations just as Judas did and look what happened to him! There are times that I have to stop and remember that I am a child of God and not succumb to Satan's temptations.

PRAYER: Lord, help us to always remember who we are and whose we are. Help me to recognize when Satan is tempting me and say to Satan, "Away with you, Satan. I am God's child and you aren't going to take that away from me." AMEN.

RUN

When Jesus was convicted and sentenced to be crucified, the disciples ran and hid from the authorities, fearing that they too would face the same death as Jesus. How many times do we also run when we are faced with adversity? When we are faced with challenging health issues, financial problems, family problems, or any other trouble, we also are faced with a decision about how we deal with these challenges. We may choose to run from our Lord and Savior or run to Him. We were given free will to make that choice. As for me, when faced with challenges out of my control, I choose to run to Jesus, knowing that He will walk with me along whatever path I may be on.

When Mary encountered the risen Jesus at the tomb, she ran to tell everyone in her path that "He is risen!" This Easter season, I challenge myself and you to run and share the Good News that "Christ is risen!" with all those you encounter. We should also run to Jesus when adversities arise in our lives. Jesus is the only one who will never run from us!

PRAYER: Help us to proclaim every day that "Christ is risen" in all we do and continually run to Him when we are faced with trials of our own. Jesus is always waiting for us with open arms. Run into His arms for comfort in times of difficulty, not away from Him. AMEN.

MARY AT THE CROSS

LUKE 2:19 (NIV) *But Mary treasured up all these things and pondered them in her heart.*

JOHN 19:25-27 (NIV) *Near the cross of Jesus stood his mother, his mother's sister, Mary the wife of Clopas, and Mary Magdalene. When Jesus saw his mother there, and the disciple whom he loved standing nearby, he said to her, "Woman, here is your son," and to the disciple, "Here is your mother." From that time on, this disciple took her into his home.*

As Mary stands at the cross, watching her son, Jesus, dying for all our sins, she remembers the events of their lives which she has treasured all those years and ponders them over and over as she pours out her heart to him.

This is my son I've raised, the son I hadn't planned for at that time. An angel appeared and told me that I was to give birth to God's own Son! I knew you were special from that moment on, but didn't know how special you would be to so many, or what it meant to be the mother of God's Son. I remember watching you take your first breath, and now I am watching you breathe your last. I watched you take your first steps, play with your brothers and sisters and friends, work and learn the carpenter's trade with Joseph.

There was that day we lost you when you were twelve and we were returning from the Temple and found you back in Jerusalem among the teachers listening and asking questions. When we asked you why you had not left with us, you replied that you were "about my Father's business." We knew you were special, but didn't really understand what that meant — and still sometimes it is hard to comprehend. I remember when you performed your first miracle at that wedding feast in Cana. Then when John baptized you and the Heavens opened and God confirmed that this was his Son, in whom He was well pleased.

You left home to do the work of your Heavenly Father. How I worried about you when you were gone those days and weeks at a time, traveling the countryside preaching and proclaiming the "Good News," healing the sick, comforting the hurting, and grieving over your friend Lazarus. Now I am the grieving one, left to feed the hungry and give hope to the lost. You never turned away from those society looked down upon; you included anyone who would listen. Then there were those who opposed you and sought to harm you because you dared to call yourself God's Son. I have known in my heart who you are since you were born, but it is hard to believe that people have had their way and now you are hanging from a cross because you dared to do your Father's will. How you must have felt to have been rejected even in our own hometown when all you wanted to do was show us a better way of life - a life of goodness and mercy from our Heavenly Father!

Now as you hang there, you are still teaching us. You have the energy and love for all of us to forgive those who would do harm to you; you forgave that criminal hanging beside you and told him he'd be with you in paradise today. Now you are still caring for me through your words, "Woman, behold your son" and "Behold your mother" to John. What love! I can't believe I am losing my first child, the one I have loved since that angel first appeared years ago, announcing your conception. How scared and honored I was! What would people say — a peasant girl, pregnant and not married! My beloved, Joseph, didn't turn on me. He had planned to put me away quietly to protect me, until the angel appeared to him as well. Then there were those shepherds and wise men who came from who knows where to pay homage to you in that lowly stable. How did they know about you and how to find us? Imagine the Son of God being born in a stable! Then Joseph was warned not to go back home, so he took us to a place where we would be safe from King Herod.

As I stand here now, I remember those words that Simeon said when you were presented at the Temple, "and a sword shall pierce through your own soul also." I feel that sword piercing me now.

What will I do? What will all of us do without you? Then there's John. You didn't overlook either of us in your agony and suffering. You are still caring for me as your mother and giving me John to love as well. Oh, how I will miss you! You told us that you were going back to your Father, but I couldn't comprehend what you meant. Now I am trying to put the pieces together. I knew that you would die and leave us, but why so soon? You are still so young and just beginning your ministry! A mother is not supposed to lose her children so young. Why did this have to happen to you? Why did you have to die like this?'"

PRAYER: As we reflect upon Your life, Jesus, we feel some of the same pain Mary did standing there looking at You as You breathed Your last breath. Help us to always remember the suffering You endured to save us from our sins. You truly are God's own Son! AMEN.

MEMORIAL DAY

I JOHN 3:16 (NIV) *This is how we know what love is: Jesus Christ laid down his life for us. And we ought to lay down our lives for our brothers and sisters.*

Memorial Day has been set aside to honor those who have given their lives while serving in the United States Military so we may enjoy the freedoms we have today. The celebration began after the Civil War in this country and continues today. Celebrations across the country honor our fallen brave men and women who willingly gave their lives both here and in countries around the world to preserve the country we love so dearly. To some it may be just another holiday and day off from work, but to most of us it is a day to honor our family members and friends who gave their all.

One of the most somber moments of the day is when our President honors those countrymen and women at the Tomb of the Unknown Soldier at Arlington National Cemetery. Seeing all the tombstones of these brave men and women who have defended our country for over 150 years and whose remains are buried in this hallowed area makes me realize how dedicated they were, and reminds me of Jesus' life. He came into this world to serve and to save all of us, not by being a mighty warrior, but by being a humble servant. Many of these men and women were also humble servants, whose bravery and willingness to give their all we honor. They laid down their lives for all of us just as Jesus taught us to do.

May God bless all those who have gone before us and their families who lost their loved ones to make our lives and country what it is today!

PRAYER: May we never forget those who have gone before us and given their all for our country, and for those who are currently serving to protect us. In Jesus' name, AMEN.

FOURTH OF JULY

LUKE 12:48 (NIV) *When someone has been given much, much will be required in return; and when someone has been entrusted with much, even more will be required.*

As we celebrate the Fourth of July, we remember back to 1776 when the brave founders of our country signed the Declaration of Independence and the United States of America came into being. In 2026, this country will celebrate two hundred fifty years of being "the land of the free and the home of the brave."

As I think about the Fourth of July, I am amazed how the Continental Army fought the mighty British Army to free this country from the demands of Britain. I think of George Washington and his army struggling to survive at Valley Forge under the conditions they were forced to endure in the winter of 1777. With the same faith in God of our founding fathers, our soldiers prevailed to bring this country the freedom we enjoy today as the United States of America, fifty states strong.

Over the last nearly two hundred fifty years, this country has been able to succeed and prevail against many other nations who would destroy not only this country and its people, but others as well. Just in the last century, we fought for the freedom of those dominated by the Hitler regime over much of Europe and in parts of Asia. We fought for freedom against the North Koreans, the North Vietnamese, and other countries in the Middle East. All these countries have wanted to do harm both to our country and others around them.

No country has amassed so much and given so much to others as has the United States of America. We are truly "one Nation under God, indivisible, with liberty and justice for all." I am proud to be an American and know that God is in control of this country.

PRAYER: Lord, continue to look upon this Nation with Your grace, that we may continue to be a leader of the free world and help struggling countries who are faced with tyrants who wish to destroy them. Let us continue to help those who can't help themselves. In Jesus name we pray, AMEN.

SEPTEMBER 11, 2001

JOHN 11:35 (NIV) *Jesus wept.*

The weather was great, fall was just around the corner, this was my brother's birthday, and I had a light day at work. This should have been a special day for many reasons, but evil reared its ugly head and this country would never be the same. I was getting ready to go to work when my husband called to see if I had the TV on. I didn't, but promptly tuned in as he told me what was going on in our country—the United States of America was under attack!

What I saw on the TV was the first of the twin towers exploding with smoke and fire and then moments later the second tower was hit by a second plane. I watched as both towers were burning and then collapsed. The news reporters could only get so close to this terrible disaster. In the meantime, a third plane flew into the side of the Pentagon, causing fires and destruction to the center of our military operations. Then the fourth plane took off on its way to the Capitol, the White House, Camp David or a nearby nuclear facility. But something miraculous happened as a few brave passengers decided to charge into the cockpit, which had been taken over by terrorists, and prevent them from achieving its goal. The exact location of the target was still unknown. They took the plane down in a field in Pennsylvania, killing all onboard. Those brave souls sacrificed themselves and prevented even further death and destruction.

We all asked the same questions: Why was this allowed to happen? Why were the lives of so many innocent people lost—those on the planes, in the buildings, on the ground, the first responders, and many others? There is evil in this world; we can't deny that. But there were many stories of how God was present during these times. This country came together to pray and mourn for its people like never before. God was definitely with so many helping save lives that would otherwise have been lost. When the question "Where was God on 9/11?" is asked, the answer is that He was comforting His people and crying with all those who lost loved ones.

God never leaves us. He cares about each of us and hurts with us as we hurt and cries with us as Jesus did when Lazarus died.

PRAYER: Lord, we know that evil exists in this fallen world, but we also know that You are always present to comfort those who are in need. We know that evil will not prevail, and that one day You will return to take all believers home with You. Good will prevail over evil. AMEN.

THANKSGIVING

1 THESSALONIANS 5:18 (NKJV) *In everything give thanks: for this is the will of God in Christ Jesus concerning you.*

As we look forward to Thanksgiving, we traditionally give thanks for the many blessings we have received over the year, spend time with family and friends, and feast on more food than we need which frequently results in nap time. One of our pastors told us that we should become thanks-giving people every day of the year and of our lives, not just on Thanksgiving Day.

Each day with our daily prayers we can include giving thanks to God for the following:

- **Our health:** Whatever the status of our health, we need to give thanks, knowing that God is in control and will give us the strength and grace to get through whatever lies ahead for us.
- **Our family, friends and neighbors:** Where would we be if we didn't have the love and support of our family, friends, and neighbors? We need to express our thanks to and for them throughout the year, not just at holiday times.
- **Our homes, communities, and churches:** We should also remember to give thanks for our homes, for food to eat, clothes to wear, and for a bed to sleep in at night. There are many others who do not have these basic comforts we each enjoy. We should be thankful for the communities in which we live as well. We should give thanks for our churches, their pastors and staff, and the lay leaders who teach us about the love of our Lord and Savior.
- **Our country:** We all need to give thanks for this free country in which we are privileged to live, and for its leaders. It is not perfect, nor is anything else on this Earth. We live in an imperfect world, but regardless of the imperfections, this is the best country on Earth in which to live!

- **Our God.** Most importantly, we can give thanks for a God that so loved this world that "He gave His only begotten Son, that whoever believes in Him should not perish, but have everlasting life." John 3:16 (NKJV)

PRAYER: On this Thanksgiving Day, we have so many blessing that You have bestowed on us and I am humbled to be so blessed with these riches. I thank You for my family who birthed me, raised me, and taught me so many lessons in life, with the greatest being a love for my Lord and Savior, and for those around me. May we never forget the greatest gift ever given --- that of Your Son Jesus Christ. In Jesus name, AMEN.

LOVE AND FAITHFULNESS

LUKE 1:30-35 (NIV) But *the angel said to her, "Do not be afraid, Mary; you have found favor with God. You will conceive and give birth to a son, and you are to call him Jesus. He will be great and will be called the Son of the Most High. The Lord God will give him the throne of his father David, and he will reign over Jacob's descendants forever; his kingdom will never end." "How will this be," Mary asked the angel, "since I am a virgin?" The angel answered, "The Holy Spirit will come on you, and the power of the Most High will overshadow you. So the holy one to be born will be called the Son of God."*

What would you have done if an angel appeared to you and told you that you were to give birth to God's Son? Mary was betrothed to Joseph, and now she was pregnant. In those times, Joseph could have had her stoned to death. Instead, an angel visited Joseph also, and he stayed with Mary, preventing any harm coming to her. What a beautiful story of love and faithfulness!

Mary and Joseph listened to God's voice and followed his directions for their lives. When the time for Jesus's birth came, a place was provided for them, humble as it was. Then when Herod ordered male babies to be killed, Joseph was directed to escape to Egypt with Mary and Jesus, where they stayed until it was safe to return to their home. From that time until Jesus was twelve years old, when we revisit the family in Jerusalem, nothing else is recorded in the Bible until Jesus began his ministry.

I wonder what happened during all those years. Did Mary or Joseph tell anyone else about what they had experienced? We do know that Jesus had siblings and I wonder if they knew who Jesus was. After Jesus began his ministry, did the siblings treat him any differently? When I think of these events, I wonder how we would have responded if Jesus were one of our siblings. Ponder that.

PRAYER: May we all work toward the love and faithfulness that we read about in Jesus' life and that of Mary and Joseph as they loved each other and were faithful to the calling of our God. AMEN.

TAKE MY MONEY

I CORINTHIANS 13:13 (NKJV) *Now abide faith, hope, love, these three; but the greatest of these is love.*

Sometimes looking through the eyes and actions of a child brings us to our knees, causing us to realize a deeper meaning of Christmas. This became evident to me many years ago when my children were young and during a period of separation and divorce.

The first Christmas after my former husband left our family, I was in financial need that I had never known before. Christmas had always been a big event in our family with lots of gifts for family, neighbors, and friends. But this year I had no money to spend. One week before Christmas, my children's father gave me some cash for the boys to buy gifts for family and friends, and a small amount for me to use.

I took my younger son shopping to buy a gift for his brother. His brother wanted a jam-box for Christmas. I found one that fit into the slim budget I had. My son told me that the one I had selected was not very good and reached into his pocket and handed me his money, saying, "Momma, here, you take the money Daddy gave me and use it to buy your gifts because I don't have as many people to buy for as you do." We then picked out a much nicer jam-box for his brother and we bought it together. We did the rest of our shopping with "our" money, purchasing small gifts for other family members. For neighbors and friends, I baked homemade goodies.

Through my son's sacrificial gift, God gave me a gift more special than anything that can be wrapped up in a box. God taught me that it isn't the size or price of the gift or the number of gifts we receive that matters. The most important thing is the love we share with each other.

When we celebrate Christmas, let us all focus on that most precious gift God gave the world with the birth of our Lord and Savior Jesus Christ.

PRAYER: God, please let us never forget the greatest gift ever given—that of Your only Son, Jesus Christ. Help us to remember the reason for the season is to remember Your gift to us rather than what we receive from our family and friends. AMEN.

Printed in the United States
by Baker & Taylor Publisher Services